To Brenda,
May God Bless You
Ellen Jean Winston
December 2015

HOSPICE
The Last Responder

Ellen J. Windham

WESTBOW
PRESS®
A DIVISION OF THOMAS NELSON
& ZONDERVAN

Copyright © 2015 Ellen J. Windham.

All rights reserved. No part of this book may be used or reproduced by any means, graphic, electronic, or mechanical, including photocopying, recording, taping or by any information storage retrieval system without the written permission of the author except in the case of brief quotations embodied in critical articles and reviews.

This book is a work of non-fiction. Unless otherwise noted, the author and the publisher make no explicit guarantees as to the accuracy of the information contained in this book and in some cases, names of people and places have been altered to protect their privacy.
Scripture taken from the New King James Version. Copyright © 1979, 1980, 1982 by Thomas Nelson, Inc. Used by permission. All rights reserved.

Scripture taken from the King James Version of the Bible.

Scripture taken from the Amplified Bible, copyright © 1954, 1958, 1962, 1964, 1965, 1987 by The Lockman Foundation. Used by permission.

WestBow Press books may be ordered through booksellers or by contacting:

WestBow Press
A Division of Thomas Nelson & Zondervan
1663 Liberty Drive
Bloomington, IN 47403
www.westbowpress.com
1 (866) 928-1240

Because of the dynamic nature of the Internet, any web addresses or links contained in this book may have changed since publication and may no longer be valid. The views expressed in this work are solely those of the author and do not necessarily reflect the views of the publisher, and the publisher hereby disclaims any responsibility for them.

Any people depicted in stock imagery provided by Thinkstock are models, and such images are being used for illustrative purposes only.
Certain stock imagery © Thinkstock.

ISBN: 978-1-5127-1858-4 (sc)
ISBN: 978-1-5127-1859-1 (hc)
ISBN: 978-1-5127-1857-7 (e)

Library of Congress Control Number: 2015918556

Print information available on the last page.

WestBow Press rev. date: 11/17/2015

To my sister, Cathy, who, in the face of sickness, has lived, cried, laughed, loved, and learned and then learned to cry more, laugh more, love more, and finally live more in the face of death on her journey in life.

Take one step and each day at a time. I love you always.

ALWAYS KEEP LEARNING.

LOVE, LAUGH, AND LIVE.

CONTENTS

Acknowledgments ix
Introduction xi

Part 1: Hospice Care 1
Chapter 1:   The Diagnosis Is Revealed, and the Journey
                  Begins 7
Chapter 2:   What Is Hospice? 11
Chapter 3:   The Stages of Grief and Ways to Cope 30
Chapter 4:   How to Find a Hospice, What Services Are
                  Available, and Who Pays 39
Chapter 5:   The Family Meeting: A Place to Call Home 44
Chapter 6:   The Estranged Family Member.........................51
Chapter 7:   An Understanding of Intimacy for the
                  Aging/Dying Patient 62
Chapter 8:   Legal Documents... 67
Chapter 9:   Preplanning the Funeral with the Loved
                  One Involved 78
Chapter 10: Medical Terminology: What in the World
                  Does That Term Mean? 109
Chapter 11: Medications Available for Adult Patients on
                  Hospice Services 121
Chapter 12: Medical Equipment and Uses Covered by
                  Medicare...154
Chapter 13: Signs and Symptoms of the Journey Home 162

Chapter 14: My Journey to Hospice 170
Chapter 15: Final Gifts from Patients and Families 181

References 185
About the Author 189

ACKNOWLEDGMENTS

I would like to thank all those who have made this book possible for me to write in an effort to help as many patients and families care for their loved ones on their final journeys home. I first and foremost want to thank my Lord and Savior Jesus Christ. If not for him, my life would not be possible—let alone this book.

All the patients and families whom I have had the privilege to care for inspired me by sharing how important it would have been to have a book like this to help them care for their loved ones.

My sister, Cathy, loves and believes in me, as I do her.

My talented niece Tiffany O'Rourke, expertise with marketing.

My children, Tina and Dan Malenfant, and Maggie Connolly, and my grandchildren, Courtney, Kaitlyn, Nathan, Emily, and Ethan, kept telling me to never give up and inspired me to complete this book.

My dear friend, soul mate and first responder, Captain Timothy P. McMahon Sr. of the Houston Fire Department, supported me with time and resources to complete the work we both believe in so much.

My new friend, Duke Rohe of MD Anderson Cancer Center, shared his inspirational writings with all of us: "Learning" and "We Never Know."

Our neighbor and friend Mr. Omar Lyle graciously assisted me with his expert technical knowledge of computers.

My dear friend and co-worker, Carmen Carreon, I have worked and learned alongside for many years.

My sincere gratitude for Madeleine Duvic, M.D., Bouthaina S. Dabaja, M.D., and Nathan Fowler, M.D., University of Texas M.D. Anderson Cancer Center, for their knowledge, compassion and time helping Cathy to take one step, each day at a time.

I would like to extend my heartfelt appreciation to AccuCare Medical Staffing of Houston, owners Stephanie Green, Romaldo Cardenas, and coordinator John Green. These people are encouraging, flexible, and supportive to all nurses who have the privilege of working for them, and they embody what an employer of hospice nurses should be.

Finally, I would like to acknowledge those individuals in nursing who are Gods foot soldiers of hospice care. Home Health Aides are on the front line of patient care and are among the most compassionate, dedicated and hard working in America.

They are the "First" Last Responders

INTRODUCTION

I read the following statement written by a man I would soon come to know as Duke Rohe. At the time, I was waiting with my sister at MD Anderson Cancer Center. As I experienced what it feels like to have someone close to me face sickness on earth and prepare for her journey home, I began to consciously learn as much as I could get my hands on and wrap my head and heart around. **Learning** is a gift that takes a concept foreign to your own thinking and makes it personally yours. It filters through the quarry of your character and your past and brings forth a life that is unique and was never there before. To learn is to be open to new thought—to be vulnerable and allow new seed to take root while taking care to filter out what is not true and not helpful. Learning is excavating an area of knowledge you enjoy and digging deeper than most go. It's becoming an authority on a matter simply because you now understand that which is still a mystery to most. Learning is an adventure of the mind that opens new possibilities in areas that formerly were believed unchangeable. The worst risk of learning is looking like a fool, which in itself is a gain—if you learn from it. To learn is to believe you can develop knowledge that others only desire to attain. It once was said that extraordinary people are simply ordinary people who do extraordinary thinking. I guess we are all candidates.

This book is about learning everything you can in a precise and condensed way. It is a book of knowledge that will help you understand that you are in control at even the most overwhelming and vulnerable time of your life. This book begins with helping you realize that we all will die someday. The most difficult parts of understanding this begin in not only the diagnosis but also the journey that follows. This book will help you turn the fear and pain of losing someone into a memorable and, yes, even joyous event for family and friends to cherish and pass on to the generations that follow.

What does the word *hospice* mean? What is it for, and who benefits from such an organization? How many hospice organizations are in the United States? How are they structured to benefit patients and families? Whom do you trust, and what are the right questions to ask the doctor to find out if this service is actually appropriate for the patient and loved one? What questions will you ask the people who represent the hospice? What do you expect from the hospice you choose? How will you understand the differences between the medications that are given to your loved one? What medications are designed to comfort your loved one? Who decides the treatment plan, and who is in charge of your loved one? What equipment is needed and provided? How is it sent to the home or facility, and who pays for it? How is hospice funded? Who decides the amount of care?

Now, as you read the following pages, I want you to educate and prepare yourself for the most stressful yet memorable experience with your loved one—from a last responder who will help guide you on the journey with the knowledge you will need. The problems in the world could be solved through, firstly, praying for direction from God and then having the common sense to educate ourselves with the truth of the particular subject. Often, we pray for direction when we are at a loss and can no longer decide what to do. We want someone else to advise us. We want to trust an authority on the subject.

Pray for Direction

Education and Common Sense

In this book, I will

- explain quality of life versus quantity of years;
- define hospice and its beginning;
- take you through the stages of grief and explain how to work through them;
- discuss how to interview the hospices;
- present how to pick the best hospice for your family out of more than 5,500 hospices in the United States;
- examine the importance of the family meeting and how to prepare the environment your loved one is in and show that laughter is also beneficial in hospice care;
- consider the sudden care of the estranged family member;
- explore benefits you can utilize under Medicare, Medicaid, the Department of Veterans Affairs, and private health insurance, including who and what can pay to help you;
- detail what every hospice is required by law to offer every patient and family, including services, medication, equipment, oxygen, and supplies for everyday use;
- state the importance of having all the documentation in order, writing the DNR, and preplanning the funeral—all of which will hopefully be early but can be a pleasant and memorable event as one of the greatest gifts your loved one can give you;
- look at the medication to help with symptoms and how each one helps; and
- tell of my journey and offer final gifts from patients and families.

PART 1

HOSPICE CARE

Hospice is a place or program that supports and cares for people with incurable diseases so they may live as fully and as comfortably for as long as possible. Hospice care neither rushes nor delays death. The interdisciplinary team approach in the more than 5,500 hospice companies in the United States is required to work and provide hope and support, not only for the loved one with the illness but for the entire family as well.

The hospice organization is also required to offer comforting care for all individuals and their families without regard to age, gender, nationality, race, creed, sexual orientation, disability, diagnosis, availability of a primary caregiver, or the ability to pay. These services are to be offered twenty-four hours a day, seven days a week, in both home- and facility-based settings by Medicare-certified hospice companies.

During the last stages of an illness and bereavement period, an interdisciplinary team consisting of patients and their families, professionals, and volunteers provide physical, social, spiritual, and emotional care. Today, hospice companies provide care to patients with any disease that is considered terminal and suspected to end the journey of life in six months or less, such as terminal cancer, heart disease, dementia, end-stage renal disease, end-stage Alzheimer's, ALS, AIDS, failure to thrive, and CVA to name a few. Regarding comfort care for symptom management, the National Hospice Palliative and Care Organization (NHPCO) asserts that no specific therapy should be excluded from consideration. The type of comfort care lies in the agreement between the individual, the physician(s), the primary caregiver, and the hospice team that the expected outcomes are relief from distressing symptoms and alleviation of pain for a more comfortable quality of life.

The terminally ill loved one and his or her family are at the forefront of care provided by the chosen hospice. The hospice has a duty to assist the entire family for as long as possible throughout their journey.

Life as a hospice nurse comes with abundant responsibilities. NHPCO has many guidelines set for hospice companies across the United States to follow. The guidelines are the same regardless of number of employees or number of patients cared for. Medicare mandates the guiding principles, setting the standard for the industry. In addition, each hospice company is responsible for ensuring that the nurses and home health aides providing care to patients receive proper training. Most of the time, on-job-training in hospice requires a registered nurse to work for one year on a medical/surgical unit and licensed vocational nurse / licensed practical nurse to work for a minimum of two years on a medical/surgical unit or in a long-term care facility.

Education in the community is vital since the purpose of hospice is so often misunderstood. There are mixed messages circulating because of the few states in America that allow physician-assisted suicide. Usually, there are two sides to every issue. This time, there is not. Hospice is not about physician-assisted suicide. Hospice attempts in every way possible for each person diagnosed with a terminal illness, regardless of age, gender, race, nationality, religion, or financial situation to complete his or her journey with the greatest comfort at home while surrounded by family. Home is wherever the patient lives. Hospice nurses will go everywhere to care for patients. *The key word here is* care, *not* kill.

Many people could benefit from the numerous services hospice care can offer if the stigma and fear of the very word were removed from the equation. The six month criterion for hospice care is an opinion of the medical community to meet the criteria, as mandated by Medicare, for insurance to provide services at no cost to the patient and family.

As you read and learn from the following pages, I want you to know that I have cared for families who were scared. They were not sure whether they were making the right decision in taking their loved one home and placed in hospice service. I will share with you what I conveyed to them: you cannot make the wrong decision for your loved one, because you do love them. Whatever you decide will be right. Trust in yourself and in God. Educating yourself with the information in this book will give you control. Always remember that the ultimate decision of life and death is God's, not man's.

What does quality of life mean to you and your family?

Ellen J. Windham

Tranquility, harmony, togetherness, and peace

Hospice

Life should not be a journey to the grave with the intention of arriving safely in a well-preserved body. Let's skid in sideways, chocolate in one hand, milk or wine in the other, body thoroughly worn out and screaming!

Woo-hoo, what a ride!

CHAPTER 1

THE DIAGNOSIS IS REVEALED, AND THE JOURNEY BEGINS

Which is more important—quality of life or the quantity of years lived?

Imagine that you are seventy-five years old and exhausted. In the past year, you have lost over 30 percent of your original weight of 265 pounds. You have a peg tube that allows for nourishment and has the semblance of keeping you alive. Most of your veins have collapsed from dehydration caused by nausea, vomiting, and diarrhea as a result of treatment intended to save your life. This journey began a year ago when you were diagnosed with cancer. Once again, you find yourself in the hospital, awaiting another major surgery in another attempt to save your life. At your side are your beloved wife of fifty-five years and your three grown children. Your five grandchildren are not allowed to be at the hospital. After all, there are rules. Your physician is not only in charge of your care but also a dear friend of the family.

Your trusted physician has kept you alive with surgery, chemotherapy, and radiation and has kept faith alive for you and your deeply loved family. He is going to do whatever it takes to keep your physical body active at whatever cost. Only one more surgery, two months of chemotherapy, and radiation should be the cure. *But wait a minute, he said that last time,* you remind yourself. The reality suddenly hits you like a speeding locomotive. The last positron emission tomography (PET) scan revealed that the cancer had spread to all your organs. How can another surgery and more chemotherapy with radiation help? Why does this doctor continue to put you through this agony? The doctor who has cared for you for so long doesn't recognize when quality of life is more important than quantity of years.

He is from the old school of medicine, when doctors were taught to believe that they must save patients' lives, and he has all the technology and control to do so. Your doctor doesn't understand that an organization created in the United States in 1974 is ready to help relieve the relentless pain and suffering and provide quality of life for your remaining time on earth. This organization can provide you with resources to help you and your loved ones cope with illness and death. He has heard of hospice but does not have the knowledge to understand its benefit to you.

A lack of education has led to a waste of precious time and endless suffering. Of course, he is also your friend and perhaps feels like he has failed you. As we travel this journey we call life, there are only two things we can be certain of. "To everything there is season, a time to every purpose under the heaven: A time to be born, and a time to die" (Ecclesiastes 3:1 KJV).

Almost 2.5 million Americans die each year from terminal illness. The majority of these people are senior citizens. Almost three-fourths die in hospitals alone and afraid. Many are kept alive for as long as possible, at all costs. These people, who once raised families and led productive lives, undergo major medical procedures and end up connected to mechanical ventilators in intensive care units, only to die after bearing unnecessary pain. There is an alternative to this physical and emotional pain for these patients and those who love them. The alternative solution is hospice care.

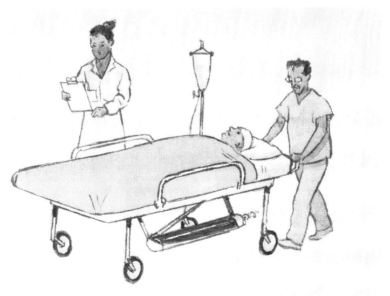

Would you rather be confined to a hospital alone and in pain?
Would you rather be pain-free and home with your precious family and pets?

CHAPTER 2

WHAT IS HOSPICE?

As of 2012, there were more than 5,500 hospice programs located in all fifty states, the District of Columbia, Puerto Rico, Guam, and the US Virgin Islands. Despite their prevalence, there are many misconceptions about the meaning of the word *hospice*. There are also many misunderstandings of what hospice is.

The word *hospice* originated from the Latin word *hospes,* meaning "host and guest." It's believed the origins of hospice came from biblical times when safe houses were a haven for travelers to rest and find refuge from bandits. The concept of hospice began in the fourth century in Rome, when a woman named Fabiola, a physician, created a place to care for the sick and dying. In 1842, a French woman, Jeanne Garnier, used the term *hospice* to identify a place to care for the terminally sick and dying. An organization called the Sisters of Charity first began implementing hospice in Ireland, work that later stretched into mainland European countries.

In 1963, British physician Dame Cicely Saunders traveled to the United States to speak about St Christopher's Hospice. The lecture was given at Yale University to students specializing in medicine, nursing, social work, and chaplaincy. This began the hospice movement in America.

Ellen J. Windham

A Time Line of the Beginning of Hospice in America

- 1974—Florence Wald, dean of the Yale School of Nursing, two pediatricians, and a chaplain started the first modern hospice in the United States in Branford, Connecticut.
- 1978—A US Department of Health, Education, and Welfare task force reported the concept of the hospice movement, which provides care for Americans with terminal illness and their families, is humane, can reduce the costs of hospital stays, and should be considered for federal support.
- 1979—The Health Care Financing Administration initiates pilot programs at twenty-six hospices across the United States to assess the care that hospices should provide and its cost-effectiveness.
- 1980—The Joint Commission on Accreditation of Healthcare Organizations (JCAHO) is awarded a grant to investigate and develop standards of care for hospice accreditation.
- 1982—A Medicare hospice benefit, the Tax Equity and Fiscal Responsibility Act of 1982, is established with a sunset provision.
- 1984—JCAHO begins hospice accreditation.
- 1986—Congress passes the Medicare hospice benefit, and it becomes permanent. States are given the option of including hospice in their Medicaid programs.
- 1991—The Commission on the Future Structure of the Veterans Health Care (the Mission Commission) releases a report with the recommendation to include hospice care in the veterans benefit package.
- 1992—Congress passes the Indian Health Care Improvement Act, calling for a hospice feasibility study.

- 1993—President Bill Clinton's health-care reform includes hospice as a nationally guaranteed benefit. Hospice becomes an accepted part of health care.
- 1994—The Healthcare Financing Administration sends out alerts regarding certification and recertification of patients. This sets off a wakeup call to hospices regarding the documentation and certification procedures necessary to avoid denied payments for noncompliance.
- 1994—Oregon voters approve the Death with Dignity Act.
- 1995—The Office of Inspector General announces Operation Restore Trust, a special program to combat waste and abuse in Medicare and Medicaid in hospice.
- 1997—Congress passes legislation to prevent taxpayer dollars from financing physician-assisted suicide. The US Supreme Court rules that mentally competent, terminally ill people do not have the constitutional right to physician-assisted suicide. The issue is left to be decided at the state level. The only state to have voted for this practice at this time is Oregon, with the Death with Dignity Act.
- 1997—The end-of-life movement brings national attention to the quality-of-life movement and the increased need for public awareness and the education of physicians. The hospice philosophy and concept of care become the model for palliative and end-of-life care.
- 1998—Hospices across the country report a decrease in the average stay on hospice due to the difficulty in determining the criteria of a stay of six months or fewer for non-cancer-related illness.
- 2000—The Duke Institute on Care at the End of Life is established.

- 2001—The Children's Project on Palliative/Hospice Services releases recommendations to improve the care of children living with life-threatening conditions.
- 2003—The US Health and Human Services Resource Administration releases *A Clinical Guide to Supportive and Palliative Care for HIV/AIDS* at a global pandemic conference held at the White House.
- 2003—The Family Evaluation of the Hospice Care Survey is launched on the World Wide Web.
- 2004—The nation's hospices serve more than one million Americans with terminal illnesses.
- 2005—The Department of Veterans Affairs releases the report *VA Transforms End-of-Life Care for Veterans.*
- 2005—National discussion is initiated on the importance of advanced directives planning as the case of Terri Schiavo, who died in Florida, escalates in the media and in public policy debates.
- 2005—The Diana, Princess of Wales Memorial Fund and the Franklin Mint make a donation of $3.35 million to support and promote better end-of-life care.
- 2005—The American Heart Association and the American College of Cardiology release new guidelines about treating heart failure that include recommendations that hospice care education be provided early in the course of the illness.
- 2006—The inaugural World Hospice and Palliative Care Day occurs with events held in seventy countries.
- 2006—The American Board of Specialties recognizes hospice and palliative medicine as a medical specialty.
- 2007—The Alliance for Care at the End of Life, a 501c4 organization, is created to provide the hospice community with a strong voice on Capitol Hill.

- 2008—Voters in the state of Washington pass the Death with Dignity Act.
- 2009—*Quality Guidelines for Hospice and End-of-Life Care in Correctional Settings* is published.
- 2010—The Department of Veterans Affairs and the National Hospice and Palliative Care Organization launch We Honor Veterans, a program designed to improve the care of veterans with terminal illnesses.
- 2010—The Patient Protection and Affordable Care Act requires state Medicaid programs to allow children with life-limiting illness to receive both hospice care and curative treatment.
- 2013—Voters in the state of Vermont pass the Death with Dignity Act.

In 1982, legislation was passed by Congress to provide reimbursements to hospices for services to care for patients. The many places, hospice care that can be provided consists of the home, assisted-living facilities, personal home care, and nursing homes. Patients on hospice services receive care from an interdisciplinary team. The first and most important part of the team is the patient and family. The rest of the team consists of doctors, nurses, social workers, chaplains and home health aides. In addition to these services, the patient also qualifies for a team within the hospice called a continuous care staff. This is twenty-four-hour care in the home at patients' bedside to manage crisis symptoms the patient may be experiencing until symptoms are relieved and the patient is at ease.

Hospice is a team of caring and compassionate people who want to provide the very best care possible to all patients and families. They are responsible for helping a family during the most stressful time of their lives. It is an approach of helping people to live the rest of their lives at home with family and friends, wherever home may be. Home may be in their house, an assisted-living facility, a personal-care home, or a nursing home. The patient will be kept in the least amount of discomfort and pain possible for as long as possible—one step at a time.

There are many reasons an individual chooses to become a hospice employee. Most of the time, the individual has experienced a member of their family or a very dear friend needing the service and was so moved that he or she decided to give back through as a nurse, physician, social worker, or chaplain. Some people become involved as a volunteer. The volunteers are the backbone of the many hospice organizations, and it is very important for each hospice to have enough volunteers to address the needs of all the patients on service. The hospice team is defined as follows.

The hospice liaison/marketer is the first person your physician may see when you are faced with a terminal illness in your life. Every hospice has a marketing and sales staff. There are currently more than 5,500 hospice organizations in the United States, ranging in size from small local hospice companies to national ones. The hospice liaison/marketer works as closely as possible with the decision makers of the facility to build a positive reputation and ensure that a referral to their hospice will be made.

The admission nurse is usually a registered nurse and will be the person who visits the patient and family when the initial call is made for a referral, which must be from a physician. The admission of the patient and family will involve consent forms to sign with the hospice service.

The patient is the person undergoing medical care. The patient is at the top of the hospice model and is a mother, father, son, daughter, sister, brother, grandfather, grandmother, uncle, aunt, cousin, and/or friend.

The family is the second-in-command when the loved one is no longer able to speak for him- or herself. The family will speak for the loved one and let the team working for the hospice they hired know the wishes of their loved one and themselves.

The general manager usually has a bachelor's degree or an MBA. In smaller organizations, a clinical nurse sometimes holds this position; however, in larger hospices, are the general manager usually has experience in several areas. This person will usually implement the company's systems, policies, and standards, ensures that the hospice meets and exceeds all applicable regulatory requirements of relevant agencies, and assumes responsibility for the readiness of the hospice to meet all inspections, surveys, and reviews, including state licensure, federal certifications, and accreditations.

The medical director is a physician who is licensed in the state of practice. Every hospice must have a medical director, whose responsibility is for the initial face-to-face encounter to certify the terminal illness as required in 1814(a) (7) (D) (i) of the Social Security Act.

The chaplain, also referred to as a spiritual counselor, usually has a bachelor's degree in religious studies and a master's degree in theology or divinity. The hospice chaplain does not replace the clergy of the family's local church. Instead, he or she assists with support for the patient and family whenever needed. This also includes needs such as housing, utilities, food, and assistance with funeral services.

The hospice social worker generally has a master's degree and is responsible for assessing the environment of the patient and family and presenting to the team any needs that may require intervention and that can be presented to the hospice team to provide for physical, psychosocial, or spiritual needs. It is often the social worker who will work closely with the family to ensure the hierarchy of needs is met for the patient and family. Some of these include assistance with housing, food, and utilities. The social worker makes certain that all important documentation is in order for the patient and family (Documentation will be discussed later in this book). The responsibilities of the social worker also include assisting the family with finding the appropriate funeral home, if needed.

The bereavement coordinator assists with improving the quality of life of the family once the death of the loved one has occurred and assesses the grieving risks involved for a family. The number of life losses in the past year before the news of another terminal illness can put a family at risk and necessitate additional assistance, with follow-up counseling for thirteen months after the loss.

The volunteer coordinator is in charge of recruiting and training volunteers for the hospice. This individual meets each week with the home health aides, nurses, doctor, social worker, bereavement counselor, and chaplain to discuss what the patient needs, whether a volunteer would be beneficial, and who would be the best fit for the patient and family.

The team manager usually has a bachelor's or master's degree in nursing and typically coordinates a collaborative hospice care team. The team may include the team doctor, social worker, chaplain, registered nurse, case manager, and home health aide assigned to the patient.

The case manager, usually a registered nurse, is assigned to the patient after admission to the hospice. The case manager must visit the patient for the first time within twenty-four hours of admission. He or she coordinates the efforts of medical and nursing team members to provide appropriate care and addresses the needs of the family through education efforts.

The hospice aide's responsibilities include bathing and hygiene, hair and nail care, dress, assistance with ambulation and transfer to different areas of the home, linen change, range of motion exercising, light meal preparation, and light housekeeping. The home health aide is a very valuable asset to the patient and family.

Volunteers are people from all walks of life and range in age from eighteen to one hundred. A volunteer is given the same background check as an employee of the hospice company. The volunteer may perform any of a variety of services for the patient and/or family. The volunteer can sit with a patient to give the family a chance to run errands or read, play cards, or watch television with the patient.

When a patient has a new medical symptom that requires immediate attention the individual will receive continuous bedside hospice care consisting of nursing care. Continuous care is offered during brief periods of crisis and only when necessary to maintain the terminally ill patient at home. Continuous care is often misunderstood by the family, so I would like to explain this in more detail at this time. Continuous care is approved by a hospice physician for bedside nursing care to manage symptoms at times of crisis. This can include increased temperature, increased pain, nausea or vomiting, extreme agitation, seizures, respiratory distress, or caregiver distress. Legally, continuous care can be provided by nursing staff at a minimum of eight hours per twenty-four-hour day. Most of the time, continuous care is provided in twenty-four-hour increments, and the RN must complete an assessment each twenty-four-hour period. The rules are set by Medicare and must be followed very strictly. Unfortunately, unless there is a major symptom to manage or the caregiver is in distress, continuous care will not be approved. This is why it is important to record what each hospice promises you so you can refer back to it.

Hospice services care for any person who is diagnosed by two physicians to be terminally ill with an approximate time of six months or less to live. This criterion is set by Medicare and is covered under Medicare Part A. After the patient's doctor and the hospice medical director certify the person is terminally ill and in all probability has six months or less to live, the patient signs a statement choosing hospice care instead of routine Medicare or other insurance-covered benefits for their terminal illness.

Medicare will still pay for covered benefits for any other health problems that are not related to the terminal illness. In order to receive Medicare benefits the chosen hospice must always be Medicare approved. Medicare, Medicaid, and private insurance companies will cover the majority of the costs incurred for hospice services. The hospice will often accept this payment and not bill the family for additional services the insurance does not cover.

The services covered include all medical care, all medication to control pain and symptoms pertaining to the diagnosis, all equipment, including a bed, oxygen, a suction machine, bedside tables, home health aides, and homemaker services. Hospice services also include physical, occupational, and speech therapy; homemaker services; dietary counseling; and the services of social workers and chaplains to help patients and families cope with grief and loss. Respite care is also covered by Medicare Part A, Medicaid, and private insurance companies. Respite is care offered to the patient so caregivers can take a short break from the emotional and physical demands of caring for a loved one who is dying. Respite care is usually provided in an inpatient hospice setting, hospital, or nursing home.

The hardest thing for a person to hear and grasp is when a physician tells them that he or she has six months or less to live. This is also hard for the physician, who may have been treating this patient for some time. Today, the American Medical Community stands accused of prolonging life past all hope through technology (thereby extending the process of dying), of failing to respect dying patients' wishes for their own care, of making decisions based on financial considerations rather than compassion for the dying, and of failing to make full use of hospice care.

A survey conducted by the Centers for Disease Control discovered that 52,100 patients received hospice care in 1992. By 1998, there were 79,837 patients being served by three thousand hospice organizations, a 53 percent increase from 1992. "In 2005, more than 1.2 million Americans received hospice care. Only approximately one-third of cancer patients receive formal hospice care, often in the last weeks of their illnesses" (Rhymes 1996 230-6). There are also many hospice patients who fall into the category of progressive neurological illnesses, end-stage cardiac disease, end-stage renal disease, pulmonary disease, or AIDS.

A study was published in The Gerontologist designed to evaluate how nursing homes effect hospice referrals. In all, thirty-two nursing homes were involved. Investigators interviewed nursing home directors, nurses, and aides. The results told researchers some of the reasons hospice care is not utilized. None of the nursing homes had written procedures for regularly assessing the terminal status of patients or for making referrals to hospice, and none had formal protocols for communicating with doctors about patients' hospice eligibility. This further supports my assertion that hospice care remains misunderstood by many doctors and patients, despite increased awareness over the years. For this reason, the average length of hospice services is only seven to twenty-six days (Gerontologist (2008) 48 (4): 477-484).

There a many reasons a physician could be reluctant to tell a patient that nothing more can be done to save his or her life—that a cure for the illness is not possible and hospice is needed for the quality of the patient's remaining life. Among the factors is the reluctance to give up. "Recently, the American Society of Clinical Oncology acknowledged that many oncologists and other physicians regard the death of a patient as a professional failure" (ASCO 16). Some physicians believe hospice care is for the patient whose death is imminent. Some believe patients will become addicted to the medication to control pain. Some physicians believe that if they do not use every measure available to save a life, the patient or family will sue them for neglect. The many reasons given by physicians reflect how they truthfully feel. This is where we have the first problem. The quality of life of a patient is not about the physician or nurse. The feelings of the physician should not be a factor in patient care, though they are often projected onto the patient. This is especially true if the doctor-patient relationship has spanned several years.

The dilemma facing the medical profession today is when or whether to give up on treatment and tell the patient he or she is going to die. These very words go against everything doctors are taught in medical school about saving a life. How does a doctor honestly face this decision with a patient? How does he or she explain that there is nothing more he can do and then go on to convey, in a positive way, the benefits hospice services can provide? Physicians, nurses, and administrators especially must be educated about hospice services and the potential benefits to the patient and family. Patients must be referred sooner to ensure a better quality of life. Both physicians and patients need to be educated on the services available.

Physicians need to be educated on several standards of care involving the dying patient. One of the main issues is an understanding of pain and symptom management. Physicians need to understand the complex psychosocial needs of the terminally ill person and their relatives. They need to understand the spiritual phase of the person's life. Communication skills are important, as is an understanding of all ethical issues involved. Physicians need to have an understanding of bereavement care and become educated about working as part of an interdisciplinary team.

Medical staff members in nursing homes and assisted-living facilities play a vital role in recognizing a decline in the condition of a patient or resident. The staff must be able to assist with recommending hospice services in time to benefit the patient and family. Timing of referrals to hospice is of the essence when a patient is suffering. The training and education of the medical profession can provide the quality of care dying patients deserve for as long as possible.

Hospice companies, for profit or a non-profit, need to be honest about the services they are required by law to offer. Many hospice organizations will promise the patient and family anything just to get their signature on the consent form—and then, when the patient and family go home and the family needs help, phone calls are not returned. This leaves the patient and family feeling afraid, abandoned, and alone. Hospices often compete for business with a particular physician or hospital. Many patients and families believe hospice is one large organization. They do not know about the choice they have, nor does the first hospice they interview always tell them. The best interest of the patient and family should always come first.

Non-profit hospices sound like charitable organizations to many people. In my experience, I have found that while non-profit hospices do great work, they actually are not different from for profit hospices. Every hospice takes care of non-funded patients. There is a reason Medicare mandates regulations on all hospice organizations in the United States. Medicare pays a per diem on every patient admitted to hospice who qualifies for Medicare Part A. The Medicaid hospice payment is calculated based on the yearly rates Medicare has established. The same dollar amount is paid to for profit and non-profit hospices. Since approximately 90 percent of patients in hospice receive Medicare/Medicaid, this can add up to a significant amount of money for both.

Joint Commission, formerly the Joint Commission on Accreditation of Healthcare Organizations, is an independent non-profit organization founded in 1951. "The Joint Commission evaluates and accredits more than 20,000 health care organizations and programs in the United States"(JCAHO 2008). It is the nation's oldest and largest standard-setting and accrediting body in health care. To earn and maintain the Joint Commission's Gold Seal of Approval, an organization must undergo on-site survey at least every three years. "This organization is governed by a Board of Commissioners that includes physicians, nurses, employers, a labor representative, health plan leaders, quality experts, ethicists, a consumer advocate and educators"(JCAHO 2008).

The mission of this organization is "to continuously improve the safety and quality of care provided to the public through the provision of health care accreditation and related services that support performance improvement in health care organizations." Its vision is that "all people always experience the safest, highest quality, best-value health care across all settings" (JCAHO 2008). In 1999, the Centers for Medicare and Medicaid Services approved this organization's application for hospice status. This means that any hospice that obtains this accreditation is held to the highest standards of patient care with unannounced inspections to ensure compliance. When a hospice has JCAHO approval, the medical community and the United States government knows that the hospice's first priority is quality care of the patient and family.

If the hospice company you choose is JCAHO accredited, the following is your contact information.

Website: http://www.jointcommission.org/report_a_complaint.aspx?print
E-mail: complaint@jointcommision.org
Fax: 630-792-5636
Mail: Office of Quality and Patient Safety
The Joint Commission
One Renaissance Boulevard
Oakbrook Terrace, Illinois 60181

Community Health Accreditation Program (CHAP) "is an independent, nonprofit, accrediting body for community-based health care organizations, which accredits nine programs and services. As the oldest national community-based accrediting body with more than 8,300 sites currently accredited, our purpose is to define and advance the highest quality of community-based care." CHAP has regulatory authority granted to them by the Centers for Medicare and Medicaid Services to determine if they meet the CMS Conditions of Participation and Quality Standards. The program is based in Washington, DC, and is governed by a board of directors composed of sixteen members.

If the hospice company you choose is CHAP accredited, the following is your contact information.

E-mail: complaints@chapinc.org
Fax: 202-862-3419
Phone (toll-free): 800-656-9656
Phone (main): 202-862-3413
Mail: 1275 K Street NW
Suite 800
Washington, DC 2005

When someone is diagnosed with a terminal illness, he or she looks to the medical community for all the answers. The answers given to that patient and family will be the most important information the physician will provide. The medical community is required both morally and ethically to be as honest as possible regardless of the patient's age, life expectancy, or monetary worth. It is unfair to offer false hope of survival for any reason. On the other hand, it is illegal to not save a life if possible.

The quality care hospice provides to patients is not a cure for their disease, but rather an opportunity. The patient may choose to have aggressive therapy for a while. If so, then this is fine, but the patient has to be informed of the condition of their health and of the services available to them to make best decision. The choice may be to have the best quality of life, for as long as possible, at home with their family. The key word here is *choice*. The greatest gift God gives us as we journey through this life is free will. No one on this earth has the right to take this from someone. The medical community has a duty to provide it without prejudice.

I want to take this opportunity to explain some history of the Hippocratic Oath. The Hippocratic Oath is traced back to Hippocrates, who is often referred to as the father of medicine. Several versions have been written over the years. This is an important oath taken by physicians upon graduation from medical school. To do no harm and to remain pure and holy in the practice of the profession was the original message.

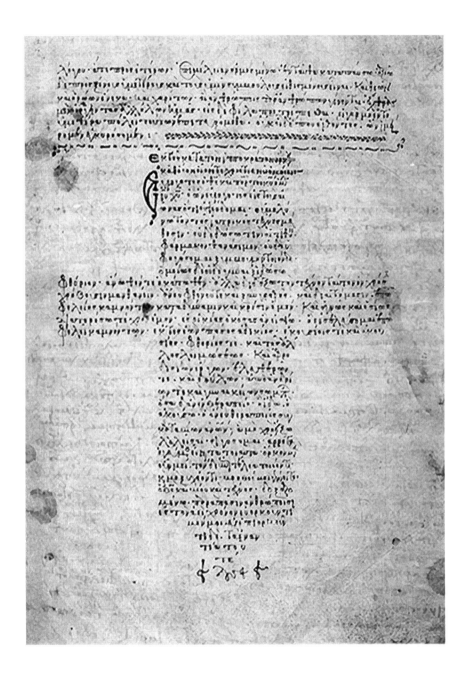

The modern version of Hippocratic Oath was revised by Louis Lasagna M.D. and appears below.

> I swear to fulfill, to the best of my ability and judgment, this covenant:
>
> I will respect the hard-won scientific gains of those physicians in whose steps I walk, and gladly share such knowledge as is mine with those who are to follow.
>
> I will apply, for the benefit of the sick, all measures which are required, avoiding those twin traps of overtreatment and therapeutic nihilism.
>
> I will remember that there is art to medicine as well as science, that warmth, sympathy, and understanding may outweigh the surgeon's knife or chemist's drug.
>
> I will not be ashamed to say "I know not," nor will I fail to call in my colleagues when the skills of another are needed for a patient's recovery.
>
> I will respect the privacy of my patients, for their problems are not disclosed to me that the world may know. Most especially must I tread with care in matters of life and death. If it is given me to save a life, all thanks. But it may also be within my power to take a life; this awesome responsibility must be faced with great humbleness and awareness of my own frailty.
>
> Above all, I must not play at God.
>
> I will remember that I do not treat a fever, chart a cancerous growth, but a sick human being, whose illness may affect the person's family and economic stability. My responsibility includes these related

problems, if I am to care adequately for the sick. I will prevent disease whenever I can, for prevention is preferable to cure.

I will remember that I remain a member of society, with special obligations to all my fellow human beings, those sound of mind and body as well as the infirm.

If I do not violate this oath, may I enjoy life and art, respected while I live and remembered with affection thereafter. May I always act so as to preserve the finest traditions of my calling and may I long experience the joy of healing those who seek my help.

CHAPTER 3

THE STAGES OF GRIEF AND WAYS TO COPE

We often hear about the five stages of grief. There are many books written on the topic by knowledgeable authors who hold degrees in all types of fields of service to humanity. The five stages of grief are denial, anger, bargaining, depression, and acceptance. Some people will go through these stages many times during the initial time of devastating news of the illness and impending death of a loved one.

In truth, they mean more than that. The stages of grief are a guideline used by health-care professionals to help you understand how and why you are feeling the way you are. The five stages of grief are there to give you permission to feel a certain way. I believe we will all look and feel differently, often dependent upon what we or our loved ones are going through. It takes a very strong person of faith to say, enough is enough. I feel I have completed my mission and am ready when God says it is time to go home.

The most important thing to remember when you are grieving is that you have the right to feel and grieve in any way you see fit for yourself. Each person is unique and will grieve the way they are feeling inside. This applies to adults and children. The grief cycle model was first published *On Death and Dying* by Elizabeth Kubler-Ross, Swiss psychiatrist.

This doctor spent many hours comforting terminally ill patients. The original grief cycle was misunderstood. It was meant for the patients themselves. We now know this revolutionary grief model can help the dying person's family and friends just as much. Often, the patient will come to acceptance sooner and more easily than the family. Many times, when this happens, the patient will worry about the loved ones they must leave behind. There often isn't a way for families to avoid the stages of grief. Most well-meaning friends and nurses will use clichés at this time to help you through.

Denial

Here are some ways denial can take shape in one's thoughts: "This cannot be happening to me!" "I do not feel sick at all, I feel fine." "This is a mistake—they must have my blood work and biopsies mixed up with someone else's." By one definition, "denial is a conscious or unconscious refusal to accept facts, information, or reality relating to the situation" (Kubler-Ross 1969).

Anger

This stage can manifest in different ways. "Why did this happen to me?" "Who is to blame for this?" "But I always try to do the right thing and to never hurt anyone." People dealing with emotional upset can be angry with themselves and with others—especially those close to them. People in this state will lash out at the people they love the most and who love them, because they know those people will always love them no matter what. Love is the one thing that is unconditional.

Bargaining

This step occurs when people, especially those who are facing death, attempt to bargain with God—an example of a bargaining thought is "Please, just let me live until my grandson's birth." The people facing less serious situations can bargain a compromise. Bargaining rarely provides a sustainable solution, especially if it is a matter of life and death. I have seen this work, though.

Hospice

STAY A LITTLE LONGER.
GO TO THE LIGHT.
IT IS TIME.

Depression

This state is also referred to as preparatory grieving. "I am too sad to do anything." In a way, depression is a dress rehearsal or practice run for the aftermath, although this stage can mean different things, depending on whom it involves. It's natural to feel sadness, regret, fear, uncertainty, and so forth. It shows the person has at least begun to accept reality.

Acceptance

This stage is reached when one is at peace with what is coming. Again, this state will vary according to the person's situation, although broadly, it is an indication that there is some emotional detachment and objectivity. People dying can enter this stage a long time before the people they leave behind, who must necessarily pass through their own individual stages of dealing with grief.

Please remember you may go through each stage several times, and that is completely all right. There is not a guide to tell you how to grieve. Grieving is a personal experience for each one of us. This is merely a guideline to refer to.

I personally believe, through my experience with patients and families, that one of the best ways to grieve at the loved one's bedside is to talk about his or her life. Laugh and remember the good times. Share everything about your future and theirs. If your loved one asks you if you know how much longer they have, tell them they are fine today. When the time gets closer—and it may be in a year—they will be too sleepy to ask. Don't focus on the illness or on time. You could miss something special.

MAKE FLASH CARDS TO SHOW HOW YOU FEEL.

DENIAL

ANGER

BARGAINING

DEPRESSION

ACCEPTANCE

Hospice

THE GRIEVING PYRAMID
ONE DAY AT A TIME
HOW TO COPE

Find your happy place.
Take a deep breath, and count to ten at least one hundred times.

Family
Have daily support.
Think happy thoughts.
Relax and take another deep breath.
Take a bubble bath, and watch a funny movie.

Eat foods you love, and then exercise.
Help someone in greater need than you.

CHAPTER 4

HOW TO FIND A HOSPICE, WHAT SERVICES ARE AVAILABLE, AND WHO PAYS

You are by now completely overwhelmed with grief and fatigue, which is adding to your feelings of hopelessness. How in the world do you pick a hospice? What questions do you ask to know the organization you choose can be trusted to be there when you need them as they promise? Tell the hospital or facility you would like to interview at least three hospice organizations.

I am going to give you some questions to ask. Then, I will ask you to add any questions you think of that would pertain to your individual family. Write down the answers as soon as you get them. You may even want to record your conversation—you will not be able to remember who said what, and you may make a decision based solely on emotion. Most cell phones today can record. Trust your own good judgment, not a referral. We are all different, and you know your loved one better than anyone.

Make everyone in the medical community listen to you.

Is the hospice program certified by the state and federal governments?

How does the hospice provider train the caregivers to care for the patient at home?

Can we keep our attending doctor? How will the hospice doctor work with him?

Does this hospital or facility have a physician on staff?

How many patients are assigned to each member of the hospice team?

How often will the hospice staff meet with us to discuss our care?

Who from the hospice staff will be available to answer our calls 24-7?

If we need to contact our nurse, what hours will he or she be available?

What is the response time of your employees if needed in an emergency?

If my loved one has a symptom that requires twenty-four-hour continuous care, such as increased temperature, increased pain, nausea or vomiting, agitation, or anxiety, or if a caregiver experiences exhaustion, will you be there for us with a nurse to stay around the clock until it is resolved?

Do you have a hospice inpatient facility if needed, and if so, where is it located? If we need help from the chaplain or social worker is someone available during the evening hours?

Are the home health aides certified and bonded with your hospice?

What services do your volunteers provide? How are they trained and bonded? What service is provided by the hospice, and who pays for the service?

Do you accept private insurance, Medicare and Medicaid?

Will you help me if I am a Military Veteran?

Will you help me understand and prepare important papers I should safeguard such as Advanced Directives, Out of Hospital

Do Not Resuscitate (DNR) order? Will you have someone help me prepare my Last Will and Testament?

A patient's doctor and the medical director of the chosen hospice can certify that the patient has six months or less to live if the current disease runs its normal progression. The patient must sign a statement stating that he or she is choosing hospice care instead of any other treatment for the illness. (Some illnesses will still be covered under Medicare.) No matter what the final decision is, the choice is always the patient's, and the patient can change his or her mind anytime. Please note that one can change hospice providers only once during each benefit period. A benefit period is 90/90/60. The first 90 day period is 3 months and the second 90 day period is 3 months. Total this establishes the medical opinion you received from your doctors of 6 months to live. Since man is not God, you may live longer. If this is the case then every 60 days you will be reevaluated for hospice services. The sixty-day benefit period is unlimited. This is important, because although one hopes not to have to disrupt a loved one's routine by changing providers, if needs are not being met, this is an option. So even after the initial interview is completed and a consent form is signed, if one is not happy with the service, you can change to another hospice. However, it is necessary that the program be Medicare approved. Medicare will cover the hospice services that are needed to care for the patient's terminal illness and any condition related to it, including the following.

1. Doctor services, including those of the medical director and team physician
2. Nursing care, including the RN, LVN, and home health aide

3. Medical equipment, including a wheelchair, walker, mattress and bed, suction machine, nebulizer, oxygen concentrators, and portable oxygen
4. Medical supplies, including bandages, catheters, urinals, bedpans, mouth swabs, and drugs for symptom control or pain relief. Sometimes there will be a small copay.
5. Hospice aide and homemaker services
6. Physical and occupational therapy
7. Speech language pathology services
8. Social worker services
9. Dietary counseling
10. Grief and loss counseling for the patient and his or her family
11. Short-term inpatient care (for pain and symptom management)
12. Short-term respite care, for which there may be a small copay. For inpatient respite pay, that copay is usually 5 percent of the Medicare-approved amount. The hospice team can recommend and submit the patient's needs for payment.

Medicare is the federal health insurance created in 1965 to provide health coverage to Americans ages sixty-five and older and those with disabilities. Credit for the Medicare/Medicaid program goes to Presidents Harry S. Truman, John F. Kennedy, and Lyndon B. Johnson, who pushed for a national insurance program. The complete Medicare insurance package includes four main parts. This is hopefully faster and easier to read and understand than the original twenty thousand pages.

Medicare Part A, referred to as hospital insurance, is devoted to covering inpatient hospital stays in the hospital, if the stay is just one night. Part A will also cover skilled nursing facility stays, but the facility must be a skilled unit and be certified by Medicare. Home health and hospice are included in Medicare Part A but also must be Medicare certified.

Medicare Part B, referred to as medical insurance, covers outpatient expenses, including physician and nursing fees; a wide variety of medical services, such as X-rays, diagnostic tests, and renal dialysis; and some equipment.

Medicare Part C allows the beneficiaries of Medicare to receive Medicare-covered benefits through private health plans. This plan may also include some extra benefits, such as prescription medication coverage. Some coverage may be limited to a select network of providers.

Medicare Part D, or prescription drug coverage, is administered by private health-care companies to provide substantial price reductions.

Medicare Supplement Insurance, or Medigap, is supplemental coverage purchased by Medicare beneficiaries to make for deficiencies in a patient's Medicare coverage. There are fourteen plans lettered A through N. Although we know that Medicare Part A will cover hospice care for those who qualify, many family members may need this information.

Social Security Disability Benefits are available for the patient and certain family members if they have worked long enough in their lives and have a medical condition that has kept them from working for twelve months or could end in death. As soon as a patient receives a diagnosis of a terminal illness, he or she should apply for this through the following website: http://www.ssa.gov/disabilityssi/. This is not charity. If one is eligible, one has earned it. Patients should not wait until hospice services are called, if they do, then their social workers can help them.

CHAPTER 5

THE FAMILY MEETING: A PLACE TO CALL HOME

This chapter focuses on the loved one and the family decision about home. There are many important decisions to be made at this time. The process will require openness to new ideas and, most of all, honest and sincere communication with each other. Many relatives may feel differently about illness and find it hard to communicate. If you have a terminally ill loved one, just remember that this is not about you or how much you did or didn't care for your loved one. This is not about who knows more than whom. This is a collaborative meeting with people you love, and you can all put the past behind you to grasp the concept that this is about your loved one and how he or she will spend the rest of his or her life on earth.

This is about the gifts you will receive every minute of every day for the rest of your loved one's life. The importance of this is simple. You can't go back in time and get back the gifts you missed because you were too angry to do the right thing. I have seen this happen in 85 percent of the families I have cared for over the years. It is important for the loved one who is sick not to be at the first meeting so everyone will be able to be honest without causing additional stress.

Once you have met as a family, have an understanding of each other and the issues going on in your lives, and can be on the same page about care, then it is very important for the person in need of hospice care to be included in all decisions.

The following guidelines are based on my own experiences working with patients and families. Use what is helpful to you and your family, and add guidelines you think might be beneficial. Just realize that this meeting should take place within twenty-four hours of the results of your loved one's diagnosis of a terminal illness and future departure. We all realize that some family members may not be able to be physically present, as family often resides out of town or could be dealing with commitments of all types. Current technology allows many ways to include a family member.

The hospice benefit allows the patient and his or her family and friends to be in the comfort of home. It will be important to have an idea of how and where you would like things set up for your loved one. Many patients receive hospice care in their own homes or in the home of a family member. There are times when the patient's condition may require a different setting—a Medicare-approved hospice facility such as a hospital, nursing home, or any other long-term care facility. Keep in mind that there are also many personal-care homes today. These are homes in the community that are usually owned and operated by a nurse. The personal-care home is what the original nursing home was intended to be. Many are beautiful, four- to five-bedroom homes. Meals are served as a family. The cost can be an issue, because for the most part, these homes are not covered by insurance. Long-term care insurance will help defray a lot of the cost. Hospice services and home health services are also available to the residents of the personal-care home.

Often, I have found there are one or two family members who live in close proximity and can provide most of the care for the loved one. Their schedule may be more flexible than others'. This person may be the designated agent of medical power of attorney—the person who is legally able to make all decisions for patient care in the event that the loved one is unable to speak for him- or herself. It will be best if one of these individuals is designated to look at all suggestions of the family and lead all members to write down the assistance they can offer for care. Then, this person should have a meeting with the patient and let him or her have final input on what to do.

The last thing any ill family member wants to do is put a burden on their family, especially parents and their children. Parents will do anything to protect their children from burden or hurt. This is the reason to work everything out in a meeting prior to submitting the options to the family member or friend who requires extra care.

If you have this role, start with a few basics on being a good listener in your family meeting, using this book as a reference. This is about your family and making sure your loved one spends every day as meaningfully as possible.

1. Think before you speak. Often, we are so eager to share how we feel about what is the right thing to do that we come across as thinking we know what is best, regardless of anyone else in the room. Everyone cares about and loves the patient. Everyone copes with sickness and death and grieving differently. Just because we cope differently, that does not mean other people care less or have wrong ideas on what to do.
2. Listen to what is being said, one person at a time. Look at the person speaking and acknowledge and validate his or

her ideas. If you have trouble understanding what someone is trying to communicate, ask the person to explain.
3. Bring a notebook to your meeting and write down all the ideas. You will not remember later, and this is too important not to recall. Record the meeting for future reference if needed.
4. Remember—no matter what you offer the patient in the end, it will be the right thing. You love your family member and would never do anything to harm him or her.

The place you decide upon will need to be home for the person for the rest of your loved one's life. The diagnosis and how ill the family member is will determine the amount of energy he or she has. Some family members may be at home or in a nursing facility when the diagnosis is given. This is not always the amount of time some people live. Many people will live for less time, and some live longer. You must make the most of your time.

The environment is important for your loved one. The patient should be allowed to stay in his or her own bed for as long as possible. If a hospital bed is required, the place can be their bedroom or whatever room in the house they prefer. Some people, if confined to a hospital-type bed, like to be in the living room or family room, where they can visit with everyone. It is important to have family pictures in whatever room is decided upon to sleep in. The atmosphere should not be cluttered, but rather, there should be items in the room the person can see and know where they are at all times. I have met so many people who think that because they were diagnosed with a terminal illness, they are completely finished with their mission.

No Way!

Make a poster with the following and put it on the wall.

Is your job on earth complete?

Are you still alive to read this?
Then you are not finished and still have a mission!

Even if a person becomes so weak that he or she cannot get out of bed, that person still has a mission. I have been at the bedside of many patients who taught their grown children the art of dying with grace. We often do things because of the love that lives within us.

A patient I cared for many years ago was the mother of a famous author in Texas. At the end of her mother's journey home, the daughter handed me a book that she had written and given to her mom. The book's message to me read, "who taught us about the dignity of death—our love and thanks."

I want to express to you how grateful I am for the incredible privilege for all the patients I have been with as they took their last breaths. You will experience this also. Don't be afraid, it isn't actually death—it is a new birth to celebrate.

The environment will become very important to your loved one as you arrange for him or her to be comfortable and happy. If patients have everything they could possibly need, they will experience peaceful lives and, when the time comes, enjoyable journeys home. Surrounding them with beloved memories is important. Family portraits, especially of younger years, will comfort not only the individual but also the family and close friends who come to visit. Sometimes seeing someone you care about with an illness can give you a sense of hopelessness. This emotion is fitting for the loss you know is near. Pictures will lift your spirits as you reflect on good times.

A large print calendar next to a large wall clock is important. This should be visible as soon as your love one opens his or her eyes. The sleep/wake cycle is so confused in a person who is ill. Most people want to know the time of day or night. Having television in the room is also important, as is music the family

Hospice

member loves and a notepad for the family member to write down thoughts, if he or she has sufficient energy. Help them make and own a bucket list, which Merriam Webster's Dictionary defines as "a list of things that one has not done before but wants to do before dying." The term "bucket list" came from the phrase "to kick the bucket"—or "to die" (Bucket list, Merriam-Webster 2015).

Time flies. Get busy.

Ellen J. Windham

Make a video.

CHAPTER 6

THE ESTRANGED FAMILY MEMBER

I have often heard family members talk about that one relative who seems to have difficulty getting along with the rest of the siblings. Most families have at least one. I have some in my family. We often believe we have a very good reason for being estranged from this family member. Frequently, the person may not agree with a sibling, whether younger or older. Sometimes the estrangement may be from mistreatment as a small child, the memories of which being just too painful to be around the person. Sometimes it may be from choosing different paths in life. Whatever the reason, this chapter is about keeping an open heart and mind under certain circumstances that may arise. I will tell you my story in hopes that it will open your eyes and heart as much as it did mine.

I'll begin with my older sister. I received a phone call from my younger sister that Rusty was very sick again. She had been sick many times in her life and always seemed to recover. An older sibling then telephoned, saying that Rusty was in the hospital and was dying. This was not an unusual call from him; he had made it many times in the past to keep us informed about her illness and the care he was providing to her.

When I learned of my sister's recent hospital stay, I decided to call her. She was very sick, and tests revealed several tumors in her pancreas. I knew the news might not be good. I spoke with her and planned to see her on Sunday, April 1, 2015. My friend Timothy and I drove to the hospital in Northeast Texas. During the drive, I kept thinking about the last time I had seen my sister. The visit had taken place four years prior and was brief. She had been suffering from chronic obstructive pulmonary disease, or COPD. She was on portable oxygen, but I did not see her as terminally ill. Timothy and I had stopped to get her some necessities such as toiletries and pajamas along with a prepaid phone.

Upon our arrival at the hospital, we proceeded to the fifth floor, knocked, and opened the door. I did not even recognize my sister. She was curled up in a ball. We sat and talked for a few hours. I learned my sister was living in conditions that were detrimental to her health. She was also experiencing yellow diarrhea, itching of the skin, and severe weight loss. When the physician came into the room, I asked to see her chart, the seriousness of her illness was revealed. Not only was her pancreas filled with complex tumors, most likely malignant, but she was in respiratory and heart failure. The physician told me the team was working on a transfer to a hospital better equipped to care for her. After discussing the options of her care, the team decided to send her back home for two weeks while she waited for an appointment at the world-renowned Texas Medical Center in Houston to discuss her plan of care. When I asked my sister what she wanted to do, she said she wanted to come home with me and be with family where she is loved. I called my youngest daughter, who works in admissions for hospice, to prepare for bringing her home. My sister was my first family member to be admitted to hospice. Although I have assisted families for over fifteen years, I had very little experience then.

There was not time for a family meeting, and Rusty had already the place. It would be my home, and only certain people would be allowed to see her at her request. All she wanted was a peaceful, clean, comfortable, and safe environment. The hospital needed to fax her history, physical, and her face sheet to the hospice. The case manager assigned to Rusty at the Northeast Texas hospital informed me that the physician would have no problem writing a referral for hospice. As I mentioned in the previous chapter, the criteria for hospice care require that two physicians must share the opinion that, based on the diagnosis and medical findings, the patient has six months or less to live—so the referral was very important. Once the nursing assessment is complete and the physician with the chosen hospice agrees, all care, including the arrival of medication, is in place. For my sister, everything, including the bed and oxygen, was complete prior to our arrival because of my daughter, who had made provisions in a room downstairs that had been the game room. There was a half bath just feet away. The room was decorated with all the comforts anyone could ever imagine. I have a great need for organization, so all of her items were placed in two four-shelf containers with rollers, which I had purchased at a local superstore for thirteen dollars a piece. There was a large table next to her bed for the medication and a notepad to track the medication given and especially anxiety and pain. Trips to the bathroom were also logged, including how many times she had a bowel movement and the movements' type and color.

She continued to have increased pain and shortness of breath, and she also continued to decline. I asked her if she felt like having her hair done and she said yes. On Good Friday, we loaded the car with oxygen and medicine and drove to my hairdresser in League City, Texas. Rusty wanted to stop at an ATM and have her own money to pay her way. She had her hair highlighted, cut, and styled for the first time in over twenty years. She was able to pay for it herself and felt more dignity than she had in a long time. We spent the weekend at the bay house with my friend Timothy, and they learned that they had gone to the same junior high. She could eat and drink everything she wanted and even had a small glass of chardonnay with her steak and potato. She was able to ride with Timothy and myself as we took a drive along the bay. We drove home Easter Sunday, and she grew weaker as time passed. She began talking to our mom and dad half the night. They had both passed on many years before. The hospice placed her on crisis care for symptom management of respiratory distress and increased pain. She kept asking to see our sister Cathy, who drove in from Austin, Texas. She then wanted to see my daughter Tina, whom she had cared for when Tina was a child. Our brother, his wife and daughter, and Tina all arrived for a visit the night prior to her death.

The next morning, I assisted the crisis care nurse with giving my sister a bed bath. Rusty began taking her final breaths. My daughters and the hospice nurse were present, as was Cathy, via FaceTime. Rusty took her last breath of this world on April 12, 2015. She took her first breath in the presence of Jesus Christ in heaven at the same calm, peaceful moment.

I was exhausted far beyond what I can put into words. What I had taken on was too much for my mind and body to understand or explain to people. All I knew was that I needed to help her, and there was no one else. I was going to do this, and I knew in my heart that God would help me. People say that he will not put any more on us than we can handle. I believe this to be true, but as I wonder, sometimes I am compelled to reflect back on where he has brought me so far. We do what he asks and don't question or try to explain how or why. He will and always does provide a way.

When you are asked to care or help care for a family member who for some reason has been estranged, ask God for guidance. I would by no means put the lives of my children or grandchildren at risk. Nor do I believe God would ever place me in that position. In this case, my sister had simply gone down a different path than Cathy and I but she did no wrong to us and we loved her.

I remember asking her one day if she would like to make a bucket list. Her response to me was her bucket list was filled. She said she only had one thing on her list and that was to be with her sister and family and to be loved. My grandchildren, who lived in the home, were four and eleven. Rusty loved how they would come into the room to see her before going off to school. Their little dog would sleep on the bed next to Rusty.

One of the greatest gifts from God is free will. He will place an opportunity in our path, but we must choose to do the right thing. I did not know how long Rusty would be with us, but God did. He wanted her to be at home, safe, loved, and surrounded by family. My sister taught me that to truly forgive is to forget the past. The short time she was back in our lives was a gift for all of us.

Ellen J. Windham

My Bucket List and My Assistant

Name _____

Assistant _____

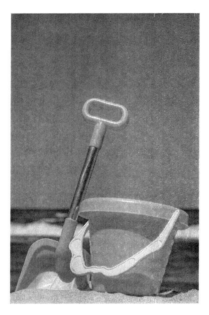

1. _____
2. _____
3. _____
4. _____
5. _____
6. _____
7. _____

8. _____

9. _____

The purpose of the bucket list is to encourage you to do everything you want to do before you leave this world. I believe we should all have a bucket list. How often do you hear of a family member, friend, or coworker who suddenly, without any warning, just dropped dead? It happens all the time. A bucket list is good for everyone to have. A family has the opportunity to work with the loved one on a bucket list and also to create lists of their own.

Laughter is one of the most important tools we have. Scientists have found that laughter is a form of internal jogging that exercises the body and stimulates the release of beneficial neurotransmitters and hormones. A positive outlook and laughter are actually good for our health, both physically and mentally. Studies have proven that adults only laugh about fifteen times a day. Children, on the other hand, laugh about four hundred times a day! It seems that as we grow up, we lose a few hundred laughs. As hard as it is sometimes, if we learn to laugh and smile again, we can have a profound and positive influence on our lives and the lives of those around us.

A pioneer in the field of laughter in medicine is a man by the name of Hunter "Patch" Adams. Inspired to become a doctor while institutionalized for depression as a teenager, Patch Adams attended medical school in the late sixties. After graduation, he formed the Gesundheit Institute, dedicated to a more connected, personalized approach to medicine. His humor-driven prescriptions and his willingness to act like a gorilla and fill a room with balloons or a bathtub with noodles can prompt a smile or a spiritual connection or simply provide a moment of pleasure from someone who desperately needs it.

Adams' method of practicing medicine has made him my hero and role model. I often have at least one of my laughter tools with me as I go to homes and medical facilities to work or to visit a friend. I am constantly searching for one person who needs laughter and can usually find them immediately. The first person is usually myself. We must learn to laugh at ourselves from time to time. Otherwise, we find ourselves taking life too seriously.

I am going to provide you with a few facts on how laughter affects our health and well-being. Then I will hopefully provide you with some tools to use with your loved ones.

The Word of God says, "A merry heart doeth good like a medicine: but a broken spirit drieth the bones" (Proverbs 17:22 KJV). Laughter removes stress hormones and boosts immune function by raising levels of T cells, disease-fighting proteins, and B cells. Laughter triggers the release of endorphins, the body's natural painkillers. A general effect of well-being is established with the release of endorphins. Laughter will engage various parts of the brain and is actually a very good cardiovascular workout. Laughter is a universal language and is highly contagious with absolutely no side effects. Given the rising cost of medicine, I feel it is important to note that laughing and creating a contagious reaction is free of charge.

Comics often use the term "comic relief." We must try to remember this when there is suffering and a desperate need for relief. Jokes are useful in defusing situations when we are nervous and emotional. Clowning around in hospitals and in hospice has convinced me that you can take humor to the deathbed. Bring humor to those around you. Decide to just be silly, and don't worry about how you look.

Practice your skill and watch the reactions of people around you. Go to the nearest costume store and buy a red nose to wear around. Rent the movie *Patch Adams*, a movie based on the doctor's life. Robin Williams had the title role and did a marvelous job. If you smile at someone, the chances are high they will laugh. They will not be able to stop themselves from laughing, because it is very contagious.

There are some extra tools needed for special occasions. The typical red nose may not be adequate. You must go to the nearest toy store and shop until you drop. You must experiment and play. Your laughter will be just as important as that of the people you are causing to laugh. A rubber cockroach or big clown shoes can often result in a smile. Toy guns that shoot bubbles work great for providing fun and laughter. Just remember that you will know what to do to make your loved ones laugh and feel better.

This topic brings me back to the environment for your terminally ill loved one and your family. Children are often afraid of things they do not understand. Know your relationship with the terminally ill loved one, make the environment child-friendly so they are not afraid to spend time with their family member. Gloves make great balloons. Decorate with cheerful colors and flowers. Ask the hospice nurse for an extra stethoscope to allow the children to listen to their heart and their loved one. Let them read stories to their loved one. Always allow the favorite pet in the room and on the bed if that is where they stayed. These little friends know something is happening. If your loved one is secure and happy then you will reflect that to the entire family and friends. Always allow family and friends to visit unless your loved one says they are too tired.

Be happy. Think happy thoughts.

There are nonprofit agencies all over America that assist families with wishes. I am going to list a few for you to contact at the end of this chapter. You can also obtain the help of the social worker or chaplain of the hospice you have chosen. I never knew these organizations existed for adults until I began my research prior to writing this book.

I can remember a beautiful ninety-year-old grandmother I recently had the privilege of caring for. As her last wish, she wanted to see her granddaughter meet a famous player with a Houston football team. My patient told me, "He is such a nice young man, and my granddaughter doesn't need his money. She makes as much as he does." As I listened to her, I began to realize there should be organizations to help with requests like this. My patient agreed, and I promised her I would include this concept in my book for all families to know how to fulfill the bucket list. She died before we could contact the team. I know in my heart this wish would have come true if we'd had more time.

I cannot stress enough the importance of doing as much as possible while there is time. I have listed a few of the national programs I could find. If you have a loved one with a wish that needs to be filled, let your social worker or chaplain know. They are always anxious to help. Sometimes long-term care facilities will have a contest for their residents with a bucket list.

Adult Wish Organizations

The Adult Wish Foundation will help grant the wishes of adults eighteen and older with terminal illnesses. This organization also supports the surviving family members to enrich their lives with respect, love, and hope. More information can be found here: http://adultwishes.org/index_2.html.

Deliver the Dream is for families of a child who develops a life-threatening disease or a parent who is diagnosed with a debilitating illness. More information can be found here: http://www.deliverthedream.org

The Dream Foundation is a national organization that grants the wishes of terminally ill adults. All adults' ages eighteen to sixty-five are eligible. This organization is staffed by a passionate group of volunteers who donate their time and talents to help make the dreams and wishes of the forgotten elderly and terminally ill adults come true. More information can be found here: http://www.dreamfoundation.org/.

The Twilight Wish Foundation aims to honor and enrich the lives of seniors through granting celebrations connecting generations. More information can be found here: http://www.twilightwish.org/

Name a Star Live, is brought to you by Space Service, Inc. They are the world leader in public participation space missions, and through this service, you can name a star for anyone you wish. More information can be found here: http://www.nameastarlive.com/

CHAPTER 7

AN UNDERSTANDING OF INTIMACY FOR THE AGING/DYING PATIENT

Imagine this scene. Anxiety builds as you and your husband of forty-five years arrive at your doctor's appointment. You know in your heart that something is very wrong. The energy level you once held no longer exists. The doctor comes into the exam room and gives you the news that brings you both to your knees. You have end-stage COPD and may have about six months to live.

Death does not discriminate against age, sex, race, religion, or economics. As we live, we must also, at the appointed time, die. No one stays on this earth forever, for death is a part of life we will all face. It is also true that no matter how we prepare, we, along with our loved ones, are never ready to say good-bye. A diagnosis of serious illness can come at any time.

Many people diagnosed with a terminal illness are over the age of fifty, but some are young. Almost three-fourths of all terminally ill people die in hospitals alone and afraid, unable to spend their remaining weeks and days in closeness with their spouse. Hospice can provide care for the dying patient and allow the patient to spend his or her remaining time at home.

Touching, such as holding hands or hugging, is a great need in all of us from the day we are born until the day we die. I know people who tell me it's been so long since others held their hands or stroked their faces.

How you choose to live your life with the time left is up to you. It is difficult for the average person to understand that the aging person needs intimacy, but seeing someone who is going to die soon is harder for some than for others. This is an area of physical and psychosocial medicine even expert physicians and pharmaceutical companies do not discuss. We will examine the importance of warmth and compassion, which continues until the day we die.

As we travel this journey we call life, there are two things we can be certain of. "To everything there is a season, a time for every purpose under heaven: A time to be born and a time to die" (Ecclesiastes 3:2 KJV). The comfort and excitement of human touch is something all people experience. At birth, the human body may perform like an instrument playing at Carnegie Hall. Each string is in tune, providing perfect harmony. The strings are protected by the outer covering of the instrument called a case to prevent damage from the elements. Eventually, with age, the instrument becomes worn and the strings break.

With terminal illness, the body begins to deteriorate, and the organs no longer function as well as they did when they were new. The covering becomes old and wrinkled. Excessive modesty may take over and prevent the spouse from feeling loved. This person may begin feeling rejected, not understanding why his or her spouse does not seem interested in hugging any longer. Appearance and grooming are important at this time. Established roles are important to maintain self-esteem. Going to the hairdresser and nail salon can lift the spirit of the aging person, especially one who is terminally ill.

A man or woman who previously worked and owned a business is especially vulnerable at this time. Day trips to check on the business will help keep enthusiasm for life alive. Visits from grandchildren can be the highlight of a grandparent's day. A child-friendly environment with balloons and stuffed animals will keep the atmosphere cheerful for the aging sick person and keep children from being afraid of equipment like oxygen and suction machines.

The need to touch and be touched is especially important to the dying patient. Specific needs may vary from person to person, depending greatly on the patient's energy levels. Often it is necessary that the patient leave the bed that had been shared throughout the marriage for additional medical comfort or safety issues. This means the patient may be placed in a hospital-type bed in the home. If the spouse requires the use of a hospital bed, the hospital bed can be placed next to the original double or queen bed, space permitting, so the spouses are near each other and can hold hands for comfort.

The couple should be helped to understand that comfort is important for any ill family member. Unless the loved one is in severe pain and requests to be left alone to sleep, holding his or her hand and stroking his or her face can be comforting. Speaking to the patient in a normal tone is appropriate. Even in a coma the person can continue to hear your voice. Hearing is known to be the last sense to leave. It is the sense that requires the least energy to use.

We are all unique, and the person diagnosed with a terminal illness is no different, regardless of age. A person who is ill can change from day to day. Some days, the loved one will have less pain and more energy. The couple should understand that holding the hand or gently touching or kissing the face of a loved one is beneficial to both of them. The hospice nurse will be able to address the issues or fears the couple may have, the most common being the fear of causing pain. The aging couple will benefit from this advice, which will fight the stigma associated with brittle bones. Privacy is another issue most couples must face, but this is especially true for the aging terminally ill person.

Friends and close family members will want to visit on a regular basis. Family members may even insist the couple move in with them, thinking they cannot take care of each other. Couples should establish a time to be alone and let family members and friends know. The spouse may be confined to an assisted living facility or nursing home. The person dying will usually be given a private room, allowing for privacy. It is very important for close family and friends to understand that the spiritual, social, and physical needs of terminally ill patients do not change simply because of an illness. The needs depend on the pain level and energy level on each particular day, which can even be true for those of us who have not been diagnosed with a terminal illness.

Your loved one will have more energy on some days than on others. Take it one day at a time. See how your loved one feels that particular day. Always ask what he or she feels like doing.

Ellen J. Windham

You may be surprised at what you hear. I know I was surprised when my sister wanted to go to the beauty shop and then spend a weekend at the bay. This was a week before her journey ended on this earth. I never would have imagined anyone could have that much strength. We never know the complete plan, but God always knows.

CHAPTER 8

LEGAL DOCUMENTS

When you hear someone bring up getting your affairs in order, that person is referring to the following documents. You should begin with making sure you have this list to go by. If some of the items do not pertain to you, then just ignore them. Otherwise, be diligent about filling out the ones needed. I have often been at the bedside of a patient who was alert and oriented upon my arrival before suddenly taking a turn for the worse and becoming unable to communicate her final wishes. Every minute is important. We will begin with legal documents.

An advanced directive is a written document that includes numerous important papers, some which may need to be notarized. The documents included in the advanced directives contain an individual's choice of medical treatment.

A living will is able to give you a voice in your own health care if you become too sick to make your own wishes known. With a living will in place, you will have your decisions about health care in place, saving your family from the stress of having to make the hard decisions about your care.

Durable power of attorney for health care is a document that lets you designate who can make medical decisions for you in the event that you are unable to make them for yourself. Please make sure that this is a person you trust to make the decision to carry out your wishes when the time comes.

General power of attorney will give someone else the authority to act on your behalf if you are unable. If at any time you can once again make decisions for yourself, this would immediately end.

Durable power of attorney allows an individual of your choice to act on your behalf for any legal issue that may arise. This document will stay in place if you become unable to make decisions for yourself.

A do-not-resuscitate order, or DNR, is a medical order written by a physician on behalf of a patient who no longer wishes to have any type of aggressive treatment. The DNR does not mean you are consenting in any way to rush the progression of death. It means your loved one does not wish to call 911 and have CPR if his or her time comes and he or she stops breathing. If you do not have these documents, they are very easy to obtain. You can ask the social worker from the facility you choose. If you have chosen a hospice provider, the social worker or chaplain can help you with these documents. By law, if there is not a signed DNR visible in the home or with the person, first responders must perform CPR. Two of the best places are on the refrigerator or on a bedroom wall, as both are highly visible.

The last will and testament is a document that you must have prior to death. All other powers of attorney are void after the patient's death. There are many places to obtain information on obtaining a will, including some reputable websites. I recently prepared a last will and testament from LegalZoom.com. This process was efficient and easy to complete from my own home and took less than a week. It was very inexpensive compared to consulting a local law firm. The team of legal experts can guide you through the process making certain everything is accurate according to the laws in your state.

Personal Records

Full Legal Name

Social Security Number

Legal Residence

Date and Place of Birth

Names and Addresses of Spouse and Children

Location of Birth Certificate

Location of Death Certificate

Location of Marriage Certificate

_____

Location of Divorce Decree

_____

Location of Citizenship

_____

Location of Adoption

_____

Employers and Dates of Employment

_____

_____

Education

_____

_____

Military Records

_____

_____

Names and Phone Numbers of Religious Contacts

_____

_____

Memberships in Groups and Awards Received

_____

_____

Names and Phone Numbers of Lawyers and Financial Advisors

_____

_____

Names and Phone Numbers of Relatives

_____

_____

Names and Phone Numbers of Close Friends

_____

_____

Names and Phone Numbers of Doctors

_____

_____

Financial Records
Sources of Income and Assets
(e.g., Pension, IRAs, 401(k)s, Interest)

_____

_____

Social Security and Medicare Information

_____

_____

Insurance Information

Life Insurance Policy Number

_____

Name and Phone number of Agent

_____

Phone Number

_____

Health Insurance Policy Number

_____

Name of Phone Number of Agent

_____

Home Insurance Policy Number

_____

Name and Phone Number of Agent

_____

Car Insurance Policy Number

_____

Name and Phone Number of Agent

_____

Bank Account Information

    Name of Bank

_____

    Type of Account

_____

    Account Number

_____

    Name of Bank

_____

Ellen J. Windham

Type of Account

_____

Account Number

_____

Name of Bank

_____

Type of Account

_____

Account Number

_____

Investment Income (Including Stocks)

_____

_____

Location of Most Recent Tax Return

_____

Liabilities, Including Property Tax, and What Is Owed to Whom and When

_____?

_____

Location of Original Deed of Trust for Home and Car Title Registration

_____

_____

Credit and Debit Card Names and Numbers

_____

_____

Location of Safe Deposit Box and Key

_____

Usernames and Passwords for Computer Accounts

_____

_____

I once cared for a lady who was what we call nonresponsive. She was basically sleeping and could not wake up. It was her transition to her new birth. She and her husband were in their seventies.

The husband was panicking, because he could not find the log-in codes for the computer, which had all of their information on it, including information pertaining to banking and household bills. The husband was missing his last gift from his wife before she died: her smile. Please get your affairs in order even if you are not sick. The only thing we do know is that we can't stay here forever. We just don't know the time of the end.

Hospice

Now and then, the great generation and baby boomers will need a little help, please. We grew up with a pencil and paper—which worked fine!

CHAPTER 9

PREPLANNING THE FUNERAL WITH THE LOVED ONE INVOLVED

Talking about and planning the funeral is consistently avoided. No one wants to lose a loved one, especially someone young. It is too hard for us to understand. We go through the grieving process over and over again and still cannot wrap our head and heart around the thought. We cannot speak to a family member about his or her funeral. I mean, how do you even start? I have been with patients and families who did not have any funeral arrangements completed when the patient died. One of the greatest gifts someone can give their family is the preplanning of their funeral.

When someone is diagnosed with a terminal illness, the funeral arrangements can be overwhelming. It is best to talk to your loved one about it. Let him or her choose what type of service to have. Anxiety and stress will greatly be decreased when the time comes to make the call to the funeral home. The funeral home your family decides to use is a personal choice. The funeral director will abide by your wishes. What you must know is that this is a very emotional time for you, and the funeral home service is a business. This is also why preplanning with your family is so important. I hope the checklist on the following pages will give you a guideline to begin to understand and complete the major aspects of funeral planning prior to the need.

If your family does not already have funeral preparations please look at the information regarding the Funeral Rule provided in this chapter and use the following information from the FTC guidelines to know the law prior to making these plans.(" As of October 9, 2015, The Federal Trade Commission listed on its website http:www.consumer.ftc.gov/articles/0300-ftc-funeral-rule".)

No one can imagine someone taking advantage of us at a time when we are at our most sensitive state. As was previously mentioned, funeral services is a business, a very large business. This is one of the reasons why the FTC decided to write guidelines for the funeral provider to comply with. The Funeral Rule became effective on April 30, 1984. The FTC revised the rule once again in 1994.

The Federal Trade Commission, or FTC, believes that when a loved one dies, grieving family members and friends often are confronted with dozens of decisions about the funeral.

Many funeral providers offer various packages of items and services for different kinds of funerals. When you arrange a funeral, you have the right to buy items and services separately. In other words, you do not have to accept a package with services you do not want. Here are some tips from the FTC to help you shop for funeral services.

Shop in advance and compare prices of at least two funeral homes.

Ask for a price list. The law requires funeral homes to give you written price lists for products and services.

Resist pressure to buy goods and services you don't really want or need or you can buy separately such as a casket or urn.

Avoid emotional overspending. It's not necessary to have the fanciest casket or the most elaborate funeral to properly honor a loved one.

Recognize your rights. Laws regarding funerals and burials may vary slightly from state to state. It's a smart move to know which goods or services the law requires you to purchase and which are optional.

Apply the same smart shopping techniques you use for other major purchases. You can save on costs by limiting the viewing to one day or one hour before the funeral and by dressing your loved one in a favorite outfit instead of costly burial clothing.

Shopping in advance is always the best approach. If you comparison shop and do not have time constraints, you will have an opportunity for family discussion, and lift some of the burden later when time is so precious and you find yourself exhausted.

The Funeral Rule makes it possible for you to choose only those goods and services you want or need and to pay only for those you select, whether you are making arrangements when a death occurs or in advance. The rule allows you to compare prices among funeral homes and makes it possible for you to select the funeral home arrangements you want. The rule does not apply to third- party sellers, such as casket or monument dealers, or to cemeteries that lack an on-site funeral home (FTC Funeral Rule 2012).

Every family is different and may wish to have a different type of funeral. There are four things that influence funeral practices: personal preferences, religious and cultural traditions, and costs. These four factors have a big influence on the type of service, viewing, and visitation. They influence whether the casket is open or closed and if the body will be cremated or buried. They also influence whether the cost of embalming will be needed. The cost of embalming can be from approximately $500.00 to as high as $1,300.00.

According to the Funeral Rule, a funeral provider must obtain permission to embalm. The funeral provider should disclose in writing that unless there is some type of special circumstance embalming is not required by state law.

A full-service funeral normally includes a viewing or visitation, a formal funeral service, the use of a hearse to transport the body to the funeral site and cemetery, and burial, entombment, or cremation of the remains. It is commonly the most expensive type of funeral. In addition to the funeral home's basic services fee, costs often include the embalming and dressing of the body, the rental of the funeral home for the viewing or service, and the use of vehicles to transport the family if they don't use their own. The costs of a casket, cemetery plot, or crypt and other funeral goods and services also must be factored in.

Direct Burial describes a service where the body is buried shortly after death, usually in a simple container. No viewing or visitation is involved, so no embalming is necessary. A memorial service may be held at the graveside or elsewhere. I have witnessed many families who elect to have a memorial service at their home. This type service is very cost effective and may be more of an appropriate celebration of life than a funeral home. Direct burial usually costs less than the "traditional" full-service funeral. Costs include the funeral home's basic services fee, as well as fees for the transportation and care of the body, the purchase of a casket or burial container, and a cemetery plot or crypt.

If direct cremation is chosen, the body is cremated shortly after death, without embalming. The cremated remains are placed in an urn or other container. No viewing or visitation is involved. The remains can be kept in the home, buried or placed in a crypt or niche in a cemetery, or buried or scattered in a favorite spot.

Direct cremation usually include the funeral home's basic services fee, as well as fees for the transportation and care of the body. A crematory fee may be included, or, if the funeral home does not own the crematory, the fee may be added on. There also will be a charge for an urn or other container. Some funeral homes will provide a container at no cost. The cost of a cemetery plot or crypt is included only if the remains are buried or entombed. Funeral providers that offer direct cremations also must offer to provide an alternative container that can be used in place of a casket.

The Funeral Rule gives you the right to:

- Buy only the funeral arrangements you want. You have the right to buy separate goods (such as caskets) and services (such as embalming or a memorial service). You do not have to accept a package that may include items you do not want.
- Get price information on the telephone. Funeral directors must give you price information on the telephone if you ask for it. You don't have to give them your name, address, or telephone number first. Although they are not required to do so, many funeral homes mail their price lists, and some post them online.
- Get a written, itemized price list when you visit a funeral home. The funeral home must give you a general price list that is yours to keep. It lists all the items and services the home offers, and the cost of each one.
- See a written casket price list before you see the actual caskets. Sometimes, detailed casket price information is included on the funeral home's general price list. More often, though, it's provided on a separate casket price list. Get the price information before you see the caskets so that

you can ask about lower-priced products that may not be on display.
- See a written outer burial container price list. Outer burial containers are not required by state law anywhere in the United States, but many cemeteries require them to prevent the grave from caving in. If the funeral home sells containers but doesn't list their prices on the general price list, you have the right to look at a separate container price list before you see the containers. If you don't see the lower-priced containers listed, ask about them.
- Receive a written statement after you decide what you want and before you pay. It should show exactly what you are buying and the cost of each item. The funeral home must give you a statement listing all goods and services you have selected, the price of each, and the total cost immediately after you make the arrangements.
- Get an explanation in the written statement from the funeral home that describes any legal cemetery or crematory requirement that requires you to buy any funeral goods or services.
- Use an alternative container instead of a casket for cremation. No state or local law requires the use of a casket for cremation. A funeral home that offers cremations must tell you that alternative containers are available and must make them available. They might be made of unfinished wood, pressed wood, fiberboard, or cardboard.
- Provide the funeral home with a casket or urn you buy elsewhere. The funeral provider cannot refuse to handle a casket or urn you bought online, at a local casket store, or somewhere else—or charge you a fee to do it. The funeral home cannot require you to be there when the casket or urn is delivered to them.

- Make funeral arrangements without embalming. No state law requires routine embalming for every death. Some states require embalming or refrigeration if the body is not buried or cremated within a certain time, but some states don't require it at all. In most cases, refrigeration is an acceptable alternative. In addition, you may choose services like direct cremation and immediate burial, which don't require any form of preservation. Many funeral homes have a policy requiring embalming if the body is to be publicly viewed, but this is not required by law in most states. Ask if the funeral home offers private family viewing without embalming. If some form of preservation is a practical necessity, ask the funeral home if refrigeration is available.

Next I will examine how to calculate the actual cost of a funeral. The funeral provider must give you an itemized statement of the total cost of the funeral goods and services you select when you are making the arrangements. If the funeral provider doesn't know the cost of the cash advance items at the time, he or she is required to give you a written good-faith estimate. This statement also must disclose any legal cemetery or crematory requirements of the specific funeral goods or services you chose.

The Funeral Rule does not require any specific format for this information. Funeral providers may include it in any document they give you at the end of your discussion about funeral arrangements.

The next section will provide an overview of the costs of specific services.

The casket is often the single most expensive item you'll buy if you plan a "traditional" full-service funeral. Caskets vary widely in style and price and are sold primarily for their visual appeal. Typically, they're constructed of metal, wood, fiberboard, fiberglass, or plastic. Although some casket costs slightly more than $700.00, some mahogany, bronze, or copper caskets sell for as much as $20,000.

When you visit a funeral home or showroom to shop for a casket, the Funeral Rule requires the funeral director to show you a list of caskets the company sells, with descriptions and prices, before showing you the caskets. Industry studies show that the average casket shopper buys one of the first three models shown, generally the middle-priced of the three.

So it's in the seller's best interest to start out by showing you higher-end models. If you haven't seen some of the lower-priced models on the price list, ask to see them, but don't be surprised if they're not displayed at all.

Traditionally, caskets have been sold only by funeral homes. But more and more, showrooms and websites operated by third-party dealers are selling caskets. You can buy a casket from one of these dealers and have it shipped directly to the funeral home. The Funeral Rule requires funeral homes to agree to use a casket you bought elsewhere, and doesn't allow them to charge you a fee for using it.

No matter where or when you're buying a casket, it's important to remember that its purpose is to provide a dignified way to move the body before burial or cremation. No casket, regardless of its qualities or cost, will preserve a body forever. Metal caskets frequently are described as "gasketed," "protective," or "sealer" caskets. These terms mean that the casket has a rubber gasket or some other feature that is designed to delay the penetration of water into the casket and prevent rust. The Funeral Rule forbids claims that these features help preserve the remains indefinitely, because they don't. They just add to the cost of the casket.

Most metal caskets are made from rolled steel of varying gauges—the lower the gauge, the thicker the steel. Some metal caskets come with a warranty for longevity. Wooden caskets generally are not gasketed and don't have a warranty for longevity. They can be hardwood like mahogany, walnut, cherry, or oak or softwood like pine. Pine caskets are a less expensive option, but funeral homes rarely display them. Manufacturers of both wooden and metal caskets usually offer warranties for workmanship and materials.

Many families who choose to have their loved ones cremated rent a casket from the funeral home for the visitation and funeral, eliminating the cost of buying one. If you opt for visitation and cremation, ask about the rental option. For those who choose a direct cremation without a viewing or another ceremony where the body is present, the funeral provider must offer an inexpensive, unfinished wood box or alternative container, a nonmetal enclosure—pressboard, cardboard or canvas—that is cremated with the body.

Under the Funeral Rule, funeral directors who offer direct cremations

- may not tell you that state or local law requires a casket for direct cremations, because none do;
- must disclose in writing your right to buy an unfinished wood box or an alternative container for a direct cremation; and
- must make an unfinished wood box or other alternative container available for direct cremations.

Burial vaults or grave liners, also known as burial containers, are commonly used in "traditional" full-service funerals. The vault or liner is placed in the ground before burial, and the casket is lowered into it at burial. The purpose is to prevent the ground from caving in as the casket deteriorates over time. A grave liner is made of reinforced concrete and will satisfy any cemetery requirement. Grave liners cover only the top and sides of the casket. A burial vault is more substantial and expensive than a grave liner. It surrounds the casket in concrete or another material and may be sold with a warranty of protective strength.

State laws do not require a vault or liner, and funeral providers may not tell you otherwise. However, keep in mind that many cemeteries require some type of outer burial container to prevent the grave from sinking in the future. Neither grave liners nor burial vaults are designed to prevent the eventual decomposition of human remains. It is illegal for funeral providers to claim that a vault will keep water, dirt, or other debris from penetrating into the casket if that's not true.

Prior to showing you any outer burial containers, a funeral provider is required to give you a list of prices and descriptions. It may be less expensive to buy an outer burial container from a third-party dealer than from a funeral home or cemetery. Compare prices from several sources before you select a model.

Preservation processes and products are also commonly used. As far back as the ancient Egyptians, people have used oils, herbs, and special body preparations to help preserve the bodies of their dead. Yet no process or products have been devised to preserve a body in the grave indefinitely. The Funeral Rule prohibits funeral providers from telling you that it can be done. For example, funeral providers may not claim that either embalming or a particular type of casket will preserve the body of the deceased for an unlimited time.

Funeral Pricing Checklist

The Federal Trade Commission recommends you make copies of this page and check with several funeral homes to compare costs. I suggest you check the online websites also.

Ellen J. Windham

"Simple" Disposition of the Remains

Immediate burial _____
Immediate cremation _____
Cost of the cremation process, if extra _____
Donation of the body to a medical school or hospital _____

"Traditional" Full-Service Burial or Cremation

Basic services fee for the funeral director and staff _____
Pickup of body _____
Embalming _____
Other preparation of body _____
Least expensive casket _____
Description, including model number _____
Outer burial container (vault) _____
Description _____
Visitation/viewing—staff and facilities _____
Funeral or memorial service—staff and facilities _____
Graveside service, including staff and equipment _____
Hearse _____
Other vehicles _____
Total _____
Other Services
Forwarding body to another funeral home _____
Receiving body from another funeral home _____

Cemetery/Mausoleum Costs

Cost of lot or crypt (if you don't already own one) _____
Perpetual care _____
Opening and closing the grave or crypt _____

Hospice

Grave liner, if required _____
Marker/monument (including setup) _____

Many people don't realize that in most states they are not legally required to use a funeral home to plan and conduct a funeral. They use this service anyway because they are often emotionally distraught over the death and do not know the legal requirements. The funeral home often provides the comfort they need. The people you will deal with in the funeral home are caring but they are business people, not clergy. People will also select a funeral home that is close to home or one the family has used in the past. Limiting the search may cost additional charges and narrow the choices of goods and services,

Comparison shopping for a funeral home provider doesn't have to be difficult, especially if it's done before the need for a funeral arises. Thinking ahead can help you make informed and thoughtful decisions about funeral arrangements. It allows you to choose the specific items you want and need and to compare the prices several funeral providers charge.

If you visit a funeral home in person, the funeral provider is required by law to give you a general price list itemizing the cost of the items and services the home offers. If the general price list does not include specific prices of caskets or outer burial containers, the law requires the funeral director to show you the price lists for those items before showing you the items.

Sometimes it's more convenient and less stressful to "price shop" funeral homes by telephone. The Funeral Rule requires funeral directors to provide price information on the phone to any caller who asks for it. In addition, many funeral homes are happy to mail you their price lists, although that is not required by law.

When comparing prices, be sure to consider the total cost of all the items together, in addition to the costs of single items. Every funeral home should have price lists that include all the items essential for the different types of arrangements it offers. Many funeral homes offer package funerals that may cost less than buying individual items or services. Offering package funerals is permitted by law, as long as an itemized price list also is provided. But you can't accurately compare total costs unless you use the price lists.

In addition, there's a trend toward consolidation in the funeral home industry, and many neighborhood funeral homes may appear to be locally owned when, in fact, they're owned by a national corporation. If this issue is important to you, you may want to ask if the funeral home is independent and locally owned.

Additional considerations include what, if any, restrictions the cemetery places on burial vaults purchased elsewhere, the type of monuments or memorials it allows, and whether flowers or other remembrances may be placed on graves.

And then there's cost. Cemetery plots can be expensive, especially in metropolitan areas. Most, but not all, cemeteries require you to purchase a grave liner, which will cost several hundred dollars. Note that there are charges—usually hundreds of dollars—to open a grave for interment and additional charges to fill it in. Continuous care of a cemetery plot sometimes is included in the purchase price, but it's important to clarify that point before you buy the site or service. If it's not included, look for a separate endowment care fee for maintenance and grounds keeping.

If you plan to bury your loved one's cremated remains in a mausoleum or columbarium, you can expect to purchase a crypt and pay opening and closing fees, as well as charges for endowment care and other services. The FTC's Funeral Rule does not cover cemeteries and mausoleums unless they sell both funeral goods and funeral services.

Now we will examine veteran cemeteries. All veterans are entitled to a free burial in a national cemetery and a grave marker. This eligibility also extends to some civilians who have provided military-related service and some Public Health Service personnel. Spouses and dependent children also are entitled to a lot and marker when buried in a national cemetery if space is available. There are no charges for opening or closing the grave, for a vault or liner, or for setting the marker in a national cemetery. The family generally is responsible for other expenses, including transportation to the cemetery. For more information, visit the Department of Veterans Affairs website at www.va.gov or write to VA Records Management Center P. O. Box 5020 St. Louis, MO 63115. Have a copy of the DD214, the separation of service document needed for all veteran rights. If you cannot find it, go to the above website or address with the information requested on the veteran. In an emergency, this can be expedited in twenty-four to forty-eight hours. They will need name, date of birth, Social Security number, branch of service, active duty dates, and the theater of service.

Many states have established veterans' cemeteries. Eligibility requirements and other details vary. Contact your state for more information.

The Department of Veterans Affairs will provide all eligible veterans with the opening and closing of the grave, a grave liner, a headstone or marker, a graveside ceremony, and burial in a national cemetery.

A horse-drawn military caisson, in honor of the heroes who have served our nation proudly

All members of the US military who served at least one term of enlistment and were separated from service under conditions other than dishonorable discharge, including members on active duty and those retired, members and former members of the Selected Reserve, and US veterans of any war are eligible. You may see ads for so-called veterans' specials by commercial cemeteries. These cemeteries sometimes offer a free plot for the veteran but charge exorbitant rates for an adjoining plot for the spouse, as well as high fees for opening and closing each grave. Evaluate the bottom-line cost to be sure the special is actually a special.

Thinking ahead can help you make informed and thoughtful decisions about funeral arrangements. It allows you to choose the specific items you want and need and compare the prices offered by several funeral providers. It also spares your survivors the stress of making these decisions under the pressure of time and strong emotions. You can make arrangements directly with a funeral establishment.

An important consideration when preplanning a funeral is where the loved one will be buried, entombed, or scattered. In the short time between the death and burial of a loved one, many family members find themselves rushing to buy a cemetery plot or grave—often without careful thought or a personal visit to the site. That's why it's in the family's best interest to buy cemetery plots before you need them.

You may wish to make decisions about your arrangements in advance but not pay for them in advance. Keep in mind that over time, prices may go up, and businesses may close or change ownership. However, in some areas with increased competition, prices may go down over time. It's a good idea to review and revise your decisions every few years and to make sure your family is aware of your wishes.

Put your preferences in writing, give copies to family members and your attorney, and keep a copy in a handy place. Don't designate your preferences in your will, because a will often is not found or read until after the funeral. And avoid putting the only copy of your preferences in a safe deposit box, because your family may have to make arrangements on a weekend or holiday, before the box can be opened.

Millions of Americans have entered into contracts to arrange their funerals and prepay some or all of the expenses involved. Laws of individual states govern the prepayment of funeral goods and services; various states have laws to help ensure that these advance payments are available to pay for the funeral products and services when they're needed. But protections vary widely from state to state, and some state laws offer little or no effective protection. Some state laws require the funeral home or cemetery to place a percentage of the prepayment in a state-regulated trust or to purchase a life insurance policy with the death benefits assigned to the funeral home or cemetery.

If you're thinking about prepaying for funeral goods and services, it's important to consider these issues before putting down any money.

- What you are paying for? Are you buying only merchandise, like a casket and vault, or are you purchasing funeral services as well?
- What happens to the money you've prepaid? States have different requirements for handling funds paid for prearranged funeral services.
- What happens to the interest income on money that is prepaid and put into a trust account?
- Are you protected if the firm you dealt with goes out of business?
- Can you cancel the contract and get a full refund if you change your mind?
- What happens if you move to a different area or die while away from home? Some prepaid funeral plans can be transferred, but often at an added cost.

Be sure to tell your family about the plans you've made; let them know where the documents are filed. If your family isn't aware that you've made plans, your wishes may not be carried out. And if family members don't know that you've prepaid the funeral costs, they could end up paying for the same arrangements.

Glossary of Funeral Terms

An alternative container is an unfinished wood box or other nonmetal receptacle without ornamentation, often made of fiberboard, pressed wood, or composition materials, and generally lower in cost than caskets.

A casket or coffin is a box or chest for burying remains.

A cemetery property is a grave, crypt, or niche.

Cemetery services include opening and closing graves, crypts or niches; setting grave liners and vaults; setting markers; and long-term maintenance of cemetery grounds and facilities.

A columbarium is a structure with niches (small spaces) for placing cremated remains in urns or other approved containers. It may be outdoors or part of a mausoleum.

Cremation is the exposure of remains and the container encasing them to extreme heat and flame and processing the resulting bone fragments to a uniform size and consistency.

A crypt is a space in a mausoleum or other building that holds cremated or whole remains. The disposition is the placement of cremated or whole remains in their final resting place.

An endowment care fund is money collected from cemetery property purchasers and placed in a trust for the maintenance and upkeep of the cemetery.

Embalm is to preserve from decay, initially by using spices and now typically by arterial injection.

Entombment is burial in a mausoleum.

A funeral ceremony is a service commemorating the deceased with the body present.

Funeral services are services provided by a funeral director and staff, which may include consulting with the family on funeral planning; transportation, shelter, refrigeration and embalming of remains; preparing and filing notices; obtaining authorizations and permits; and coordinating with the cemetery, crematory or other third parties.

A grave is a space in the ground in a cemetery for the burial of remains.

A grave liner or outer container is a concrete cover that fits over a casket in a grave. Some liners cover the top and sides of the casket. Others, referred to as vaults, completely enclose the casket. Grave liners minimize ground settling.

Graveside service is a service to commemorate the deceased held at the cemetery before burial.

Interment is burial in the ground, inurnment, or entombment.

Inurnment is the placing of cremated remains in an urn.

A mausoleum is a building in which remains are buried or entombed.

A memorial service is a ceremony commemorating the deceased without the body present and can be anywhere you decide.

A niche is a space in a columbarium, mausoleum, or niche wall to hold an urn.

An urn is a container to hold cremated remains. It can be placed in a columbarium or mausoleum or buried in the ground.

A vault is a grave liner that completely encloses a casket.

Funeral Cost Breakdown

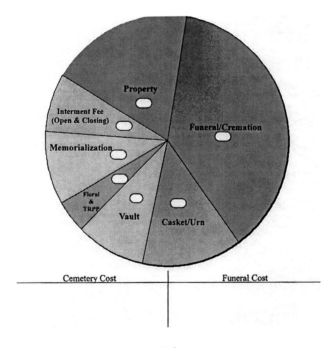

Begin with History

Name

_____

Address

_____

_____

E-mail Address

_____

Phone Number

_____

Sex

_____

Social Security Number

_____-_____-_____

Place of Birth

_____

Date of Birth

_____/_____/_____

Marital Status

_____

Date of Marriage

_____/_____/_____

Name of Surviving Spouse

_____

Occupation

_____

Business/Industry

_____

Employer

_____

Phone Number

_____

_____

Elementary/Secondary School Attended

_____

Hospice

College Attended

_____

Degrees

_____

Military Service

_____

Father's Name

_____

Father's Place of Birth

_____

Mother's First name and Maiden Name

_____

Mother's Place of Birth

_____

Name of Person Responsible for Completing Arrangements

_____

Address

_____

_____

E-mail Address

_____

Phone Number

_____

Experiences of Early Childhood

_____

_____

Experiences of Adolescence

_____

_____

Experiences of Early Adulthood

_____

_____

Hospice

Proudest Family Moments

_____

_____

Proudest Career Accomplishments

_____

_____

Favorite Songs

_____

_____

Favorite Colors

_____

_____

Hobbies

_____

_____

Things to Remember

_____

_____

Now we will examine preplanning the funeral with your loved one. By now, you have decided upon the type of funeral you and your loved one would like to have, so now comes documenting the detailed information to be included and the service itself.

Chosen Funeral Home

_____

Address

_____

_____

Phone Number

_____/_____/_____

E-mail Address

_____

Type of Service

_____

Place of Service

_____

Service Preference

_____

Hospice

Clergyman/Speaker Name

_____

Favorite Readings and Passages

_____

_____

Musicians or Musical Selections

_____

_____

Type of Casket Selected

_____

Date Selected and Prepaid

_____/_____/_____

Participating Organizations

_____

Names of Pallbearers

_____

_____

Names of Honorary Pallbearers

_____

_____

Flag Instructions

_____

Wake or Rosary

_____

Officiant

_____

Date

_____

Time

_____

Location

_____

Visitation (Public or Private)

_____

Hospice

Casket (Open or Closed)

_____

Clothing Preferences

_____

Eyeglasses to be Worn

_____

Memorial Donations to Hospice

_____

Newspaper Where Obituary Will Be Published

_____

Reception Location

_____

Additional Notes

_____

_____

_____

For more information on funeral homes and funeral home services and where to file a complaint, see the list below.

Most states have a licensing board that regulates the funeral industry. You may contact the board in your state for information or help. If you want additional information about making funeral arrangements and the options available, you may want to contact interested business, professional and consumer groups. Some of the biggest are listed here.

- AARP is a membership organization for people fifty years of age and older. Funeral-related information is available on their web site www.aarp.org/
- Cremation Association of North America is an association of crematories, cemeteries, and funeral homes that offer cremation.
- Funeral Consumers Alliance is a nonprofit educational organization that supports increased funeral consumer protection. Their website has free pamphlets on funeral planning, plus a directory of local volunteer funeral-planning groups.
- Funeral Ethics Organization (FEO) is an independent nonprofit educational organization, promotes ethical dealings in death-related transactions, and provides mediation assistance to resolve consumer complaints.
- Green Burial Council is an independent nonprofit that encourages environmentally sustainable death care practices as a means of acquiring, restoring, and stewarding natural areas and assists consumers in identifying "green" cemetery, funeral, and cremation services.
- International Cemetery, Cremation and Funeral Association (ICCFA) is a nonprofit association of cemeteries, funeral homes, crematories, and monument retailers that offers

informal mediation of consumer complaints through its Cemetery Consumer Service Council. Its website provides information and advice in its Consumer Resource Guide.
- International Order of the Golden Rule is an international association of about 1,300 independent funeral homes.
- Jewish Funeral Directors of America is an international association of funeral homes serving the Jewish community.
- The National Funeral Directors Association (NFDA) is an educational and professional association of funeral directors that provides consumer information and sponsors the NFDA Help Line, which is designed to help consumers resolve complaints about NFDA members.
- The National Funeral Directors and Morticians Association is a national association primarily of African American funeral providers.
- Selected Independent Funeral Homes is an international association of funeral firms that have agreed to comply with its Code of Good Funeral Practice.

If you have a problem concerning funeral matters, it's best to try to resolve it first with the funeral director. If you are dissatisfied with the funeral services you receive, the Funeral Consumers Alliance offers advice on how best to resolve a problem. In addition, the FEO, the NFDA Help Line, and the ICCFA Cemetery Consumer Service Council may be able to provide informal mediation of a complaint. You also can contact your state attorney general's office or local consumer protection agencies. In addition, you can file a complaint with the FTC online at www.consumer.ftc.gov/.../0300-ftc-funeral-ru...or call 1-877-FTC-HELP (382-4357) or 1-866-653-4261 (TDD). Although the commission cannot resolve individual problems for consumers, it can act against a company if it sees a pattern of possible law violations (FTC Funeral Rule 2012).

As stated earlier in this book, the hospice you choose will provide bereavement services to everyone in the family who needs help following a death. They will be in contact though the possible crisis period of thirteen months. Many will have group meetings. I was director of volunteer and bereavement services for a local hospice at one time. Meetings were held once a month for those who felt they could benefit from talking to others going through a similar experience. It helped, and we had great snacks.

CHAPTER 10

MEDICAL TERMINOLOGY: WHAT IN THE WORLD DOES THAT TERM MEAN?

I am including this chapter because medical language is often tough to understand. The reason for this is that many things are named after the physicians who discovered them. Did you know there is a class taught in medical schools called medical terminology? Here are some definitions for you to have in case they are given to you.

Abd refers to the abdomen. Also called the stomach, tummy, or midriff, this is part of the body between the thorax (chest) and pelvis. The region where the abdomen is enclosed is called the abdominal cavity.

ACLS, or advanced cardiac life support, refers to a set of clinical interventions for the treatment of cardiac arrest, stroke, and other medical emergencies.

An AED, or advanced external defibrillator, is a portable electronic device that is able to automatically diagnose the life-threatening cardiac arrhythmias of ventricular tachycardia in a patient and is able to treat them through defibrillation, the application of electrical therapy, which stops the arrhythmia, allowing the heart to reestablish an effective rhythm.

AF, a-fib, or atrial fibrillation is the most common abnormal heart rhythm. There are times when there are no obvious symptoms. It is often associated with palpitations, fainting, chest pain, or congestive heart failure. AF may be identified by taking the pulse and confirmed with an electrocardiogram.

Aggressive treatment is a method of treating a possibly life-threatening illness where every available known or experimental medication or treatment is given, hoping to achieve additional time or a cure, regardless of the side effects.

AI, or aortic insufficiency, is the leaking of the aortic valve of the heart, causing blood to flow in the reverse direction during ventricular diastole from the aorta and the left ventricle.

ALS, or advanced life support, is a set of life-saving protocols and skills that extend basic life support whose goal is to further support circulation and provide an open airway and adequate breathing.

AMA, or against medical advice, a term used in health care institutions when a patient leaves a hospital against the advice of their doctor. The ethics of a competent person making a decision about his or her own health care must always be considered. There is a widespread ethical consensus that even when patients decline a treatment recommended, health care professionals still have a duty to provide care and support to the patient and should never abandon the patient.

Apnea is a symptom where a person will stop breathing for a period of time. Five to sixty seconds could pass before a breath is taken again.

AS, or aortic stenosis, is a disease of the heart valves in which the opening of aortic valve is narrowed. The aorta, the largest artery in the body, carries the entire output of blood to the systemic circulation. Aortic stenosis is the most common heart disease involving the heart valves.

An aneurysm is a balloon-like bulge in an artery. Arteries carry oxygen-rich blood to your body. Sometimes genetic diseases will cause damage to the wall of an artery, causing blood to push against the weakened wall.

BE, or a barium enema, is a lower gastrointestinal medical procedure used to examine and diagnose problems with the colon, or large intestine. While an enema of barium sulfate is administered, a technician will take the proper amount of X-rays ordered by your physician to provide an accurate diagnosis.

BMR, or basal metabolism rate, is the rate of energy expenditure by humans at rest and is measured in kilojoules per hour per kilograms of body mass. Rest is defined as existing in a neutrally temperate environment while in a post absorptive state. The release and use of energy in this state is sufficient only for the functioning of the vital organs: the heart, lungs, nervous system, kidneys, liver, intestine, sex organs, muscles, brain, and skin.

BP, or blood pressure, is the pressure exerted by circulating blood on the walls of the blood vessels and is considered one of the vital signs. Blood pressure refers to the arterial pressure of the systemic circulation and can be measured with the person's upper arm, utilizing the brachial pulse, or a person's wrist, utilizing the radial pulse. The latter method is accurate and more comfortable.

Blood pressure will vary depending on the disease state and activity. Pain is also a factor for increased blood pressure, because it is regulated by the nervous system and the endocrine system.

Buccal is an area of the mouth just inside the cheek and is used as a route for medication to be given.

BUN, or blood urea nitrogen, is a measure of the amount of nitrogen in the blood that comes from urea. High levels can be an indication of kidney disease.

Ca, or Carcinoma, is a type of cancer that develops from epithelial cells. Carcinoma begins in a tissue that lines the inner and outer surfaces of the body and may arise from cells originating in the endodermal germ layer.

CBC, or complete blood count, is a blood test to look at the count of all types of blood cells. The blood count is one of the first indicators that a disease process is taking place in the body.

CC, or chief complaint, is the term for the main reason a person is seeking medical attention. The symptom the person is experiencing will lead the physician to discover the diagnosis.

Cheyne stokes breathing is a type of breathing at the end of life where a long, deep breath followed by short, rapid breaths.

CNS, or central nervous system, is the part of the human body that contains the brain and the spinal cord. The peripheral nervous system, or PNS, is composed of nerves, which lead to and from the CNS.

A comfort kit consists of emergency medications which should be ordered on the day the patient is admitted to hospice care and be at the destination prior to release from the hospital. Always delivered to your home. If a hospice tells you it does not deliver medication, do not sign up with it. You have enough to do.

CPR, or cardiopulmonary resuscitation, is an emergency procedure performed in an effort to manually preserve intact brain function until measures can be taken to increase blood circulation and breathing in a person who has gone into cardiac arrest. CPR is necessary for those who are nonresponsive with little or no breathing. CPR is not indicated for a person who has a known DNR.

A CVA, a cerebrovascular accident or stroke, is commonly described as a loss of brain function due to a disturbance in the blood flow to the brain. This disturbance is due to either a lack of blood flow to the brain or hemorrhage.

DD, or differential diagnosis, is a method of reducing the probabilities of a person's condition based on symptoms, past medical history provided by the patient, and medical knowledge.

DO, or doctor of osteopathic medicine, is a professional doctoral degree for physicians and surgeons offered by medical schools in the United States.

DNR, or do not resuscitate, is a legal order written either in a hospital or on a legal form to express the wishes of the patient not to undergo life-saving techniques such as CPR if the person's heart stops and/or they stop breathing. The DNR request is made by the patient or the designated medical power of attorney. The DNR must be fully filled out with the signatures of all involved, including the physician. Patients who have a DNR can change their minds at any time and can also continue to get antibiotics, chemotherapy, dialysis, and other appropriate treatments.

Dyspepsia is indigestion or an upset stomach.

Dysphagia is difficulty swallowing.

An EEG, or electroencephalogram, is a recording of electrical activity along the scalp with multiple electrodes over a short period of time, usually ten to twenty minutes. An EEG is usually preformed to diagnose epilepsy, sleep disorders, coma, and encephalopathy and to determine brain death.

Election of hospice benefit is in effect when the consent papers are signed and the patient is admitted to a particular hospice service.

An EMG, or electromyography, is a technique for evaluating and recording the electrical activity in the skeletal muscle. An instrument called an electromyography is used to make a record called an electromyogram. The electromyography records the action potential generated by the muscle cell.

EMS, or emergency medical service, is a type of emergency service that provides out-of-hospital transport to patients with illnesses who are unable to transport themselves or ride to their destination by car.

A face-to-face visit between the hospice physician or nurse practitioner and a patient occurs every sixty days to determine whether the patient is still appropriate for eligibility to be on hospice care. This visit happens once the patient has been on service longer than the initial ninety-day certification and prior to the 180-day recertification.

FBS, fasting blood sugar, is the level of sugar is in one's blood after fasting overnight. This is used to test for diabetes. The normal range for blood glucose is typically seventy to one hundred milligrams per deciliter.

The GI, or gastrointestinal, tract is an organ system responsible for consuming and digesting foods, absorbing nutrients, and expelling waste. The GI tract consists of the stomach and intestines and is divided into the upper and lower gastrointestinal tract. The GI tract begins at the mouth and ends at the anus.

The GU, or genitourinary, system refers to the reproductive and urinary systems. These systems are grouped together because of their proximity and some common pathways.

HIV/AIDS is a disease of the immune system caused by infection with the human immunodeficiency virus.

Hgb, or hemoglobin, is the iron-containing oxygen transport in red blood cells. Hemoglobin in the blood carries oxygen from the lungs throughout the body, where it releases the oxygen to burn nutrients to provide energy to power metabolism.

A hospice-appropriate patient is a person who has been diagnosed with a terminal illness and for whom two physicians have determined, based on all available reports, that *in their opinion* the person has six months (180 days) or less to live.

An IDT, or interdisciplinary team, is a group of people every patient on service with hospice has available to them. This team meets each week to discuss and resolve all concerns raised by the patient and family and includes a doctor, a team manager, an RN case manager, a home health aide, a bereavement director, a volunteer director, a social worker, and a chaplain.

Imminent death is when death is expected within one to two days.

IM, or intramuscular, describes an injection of medication directly into a muscle, the deltoid muscle in the upper arm, the vastus lateralis muscle in the leg, or the ventrogluteal and dorsogluteal muscles of the buttocks.

IPU, or inpatient unit, is a level of care where the patients' symptoms cannot be managed at home. Often when symptoms are controlled the patient will return home. The amount of beds available is dependent upon the hospice chosen.

IV, or intravenous, therapy is an infusion of liquids directly into a vein. This route of receiving medications or fluids is often called a drip. Medications and fluids have an almost immediate response with this route. This can be used for fluid replacement in the case of dehydration when the person is unable to swallow.

LOC, or level of care, is the specific level of care a patient is currently receiving. The level of care can change back and forth depending on the person's condition. Some levels include routine home care, continuous care, respite care, and inpatient care.

LPN and LVN stand for licensed practical nurse and licensed vocational nurse, respectively. The job description for both is the same and depends upon the state of practice. This is a nurse who cares for people who are sick, injured, convalescent, or disabled under the direction of a registered nurse or physician.

Medicare Hospice Benefit is a benefit that anyone who is eligible for Medicare is qualified to receive. The person must be appropriate for hospice services. The criterion is a prognosis of six months or less to live as certified by two physicians. The Medicare Hospice Benefit provides the patient with all medications, equipment, supplies, and visits and care from the staff of the hospice service they have chosen.

Mottling is when the skin has begun to turn either purple or blue in color. The cause is the lack of circulation due to a decrease in blood flow to these areas. The extremities will often turn first, the feet and knees, and then sometimes the nail beds and fingers. Mottling can come and go at different times and does not occur with everyone.

MI, or myocardial infarction, is the medical term for a heart attack. An MI happens when blood flow is actually stopped from going to any part of the heart. The heart muscle is injured. Often, an MI is caused by a blockage in one of the main arteries leading to the heart.

N, or normal, is a term often used in medicine to describe a result of a test or a state of behavior. This term is defined as "the most common for society." Everyone has a different degree of normal. *Normal* should apply to one particular person.

An on-call nurse is a hospice nurse that is available with direct access to the physician twenty-four hours a day, seven days a week. This applies to every hospice.

A PCG, or primary caregiver, is responsible for the patient and is the designated go-to person for the hospice if the patient is unable to speak for him- or herself.

pH is an expression of acidity or alkalinity. A pH of seven is neutral. Above seven, alkalinity increases; below seven, acidity increases.

PO means the medication is given to the patient with water by mouth. A person should only be given PO medicine if he or she is awake and can swallow without coughing. Also, if the person is awake, the medicine can be crushed if it is not extended release.

A POC, or plan of care, is available for every patient on service with the hospice. The plan of care is individualized to meet the needs of the patient and family.

Palliative care is a term of comfort measures.

A PSA, or prostate-specific antigen, is a glycoprotein enzyme encoded in humans by the KLK3 gene. PSA is a member of the kallikrein-related peptidase family and is secreted by the epithelial cells of the prostate gland.

A RBC, or red blood cell, is also called an erythrocyte. The detection of high or low amounts in the bloodstream will assist the physician with the proper diagnosis. The term is used in connection with a CBC, or complete blood cell count.

Recertification in the context of hospice care refers to the confirmation provided by the hospice medical director at the end of a benefit period that a patient is still terminally ill. Recertification is necessary in order for a patient to continue to receive hospice care. One can get hospice care for two ninety-day benefit periods, followed by an unlimited number of sixty-day benefit periods.

Referrals are made when the hospice staff meets with patients and families to talk about the services they will provide. A referral is usually made by a member of the hospital administrative team. Referrals are free of charge and are offered without any obligation on the patient's part to sign up with that particular hospice unless all questions are answered in writing.

Respite stay is a five-day stay used to provide rest for both the caregiver and the patient. Respite can be provided at various locations. The patient can be returned home and placed back on routine care. The respite care benefit can be used once every thirty days.

Routine home care is the level of care patients receive in their homes when the majority of symptoms are controlled.

SC, or subcutaneous, describes the lowermost layer of the skin. Subcutaneous injections are given upper arm, thigh, and abdomen.

SOB, or shortness of breath, also known as dyspnea, is the feeling associated with impaired breathing. Dyspnea is a normal symptom of heavy exertion, such as exercise or running. In regard to illness, some of the causes may be due to asthma, pneumonia, cardiac problems, chronic obstructive pulmonary disease (COPD), panic disorders, and anxiety.

Stat comes from the Latin word *statum*, meaning "instant" or "immediately."

Subq line is a small butterfly needle that is placed in the fatty tissue anywhere on the body and is simply taped into place. This is an excellent way to administer medication when the patient is unable to swallow oral medication.

Sublingual means under the tongue. This allows for medication to be given to patients in any setting.

Transdermal patch is a system of dispensing a drug through the skin—pain patch, blood pressure.

Terminal restlessness is a term used when your loved one is unable to be comfortable in bed or sit for a period of time.

Terminal secretions, sometimes referred to as the death rattle, are a sound caused by the inability to clear the accumulation of liquid in the back of the throat, which thus sometimes settles around the lungs. This occurs because the person is too weak to cough, and death usually occurs within forty-eight to seventy-two hours after secretions start.

List of Medical Abbreviations Related to Medication Administration Time and Route

Abbreviation	Meaning
a.c.	before meals
b.i.d.	twice a day
gtt	drop
h	hour
h.s.	at bedtime
N.P.O.	nothing by mouth
o.d.	right eye
o.s.	left eye
o.u.	both eyes
p.c.	after food
p.m.	afternoon
p.o.	orally/by mouth
p.r.	per rectal
p.r.n.	as needed
q.d.	every day
q.2.h.	every two hours
q.4.h.	every four hours
q.6.h	every six hours
q.8.h	every eight hours
q.a.m.	every morning
q.i.d.	four times a day
q.h.	every hour, hourly
q.s.	a sufficient quantity

Rx	prescription
Sig. or S.	directions
stat	immediately, with no delay
t.i.d. or t.d.s.	three times a day

Ask your hospice nurse for a weekly medication reminder container. Each hospice will have access to them. This is used to fill the scheduled medications for a week at a time. Medications can get confusing, and it is your hospice nurse's responsibility to help you with this.

Keep as-needed medication separate from scheduled medication.

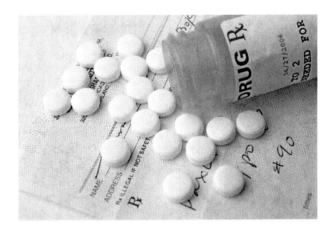

CHAPTER 11

MEDICATIONS AVAILABLE FOR ADULT PATIENTS ON HOSPICE SERVICES

The guideline that the pharmacies supplying the hospice organizations follow is that patient care should always be tailored to the individual. Every person is different. There is a standard used in hospice, but the types of medication and the dosages must be catered to that particular person, taking into account age, diagnosis, past health history, and current symptoms.

Although medication itself is very important, especially pertaining to the person's current symptom management, the types and dosages of medications are extremely important at this time as well.

A patient who is discharged from the hospital and admitted to hospice one day may experience a complete set of symptoms weeks later. It is the job of the caregiver to notify the hospice case manager of all changes in condition so the physician can adjust and in some cases change the medication or route of medication altogether. The goal of this chapter is to explain some of the medications available for your loved one if needed.

These medicines are available from the hospice pharmacies but are often not offered to the families due to cost. As long as the medication is related to the hospice diagnosis, the medication should be covered. Medication should also be prescribed very carefully to frail and older adults, particularly those with compromised liver and kidney function. I will also explain some ways to alleviate symptoms without having to medicate.

Have a notebook and write down the name of the medication, medication dosage, time given, what the medication is for and the route you are giving it. Please understand the following information is not intended to prescribe medication but rather to give you the knowledge of the types and routes available from most of the hospice pharmacies.

The Six Rights of Medication

When you are giving medication, regardless of the type, you need to always follow the six rights. Some of this medication can take the time you spend with your loved one away. Family members and professionals alike should always check twice before giving it. Each time you administer a medication, you need to be sure to have the following.

1. Right individual
2. Right medication
3. Right dose
4. Right time
5. Right route
6. Right documentation

Routes of Administration of Medication: Oral Medication (PO)

Oral administration of medication is best for the patient and the family and is the preferred method of all hospice companies as well. There may be times when this route will not work—for example, when the patient is unable to swallow due to nausea and vomiting or when there is a decrease in the level of consciousness. In these cases, the hospice is very reluctant to order the proper route of medication due to cost. The cost should never be placed above the care and comfort of the individual.

Compounding Medication

Compounding medication is the art and science of preparing medication for a patient. These medications are made from scratch. Prior to the 1950s and 1960s, all medication was made by compounding, because it was specific to the needs of individual patients. Eventually, mass production of medication became the norm, and pharmacists were no longer trained to compound. Compounding medications to be given by to the individual patient is a costly and time-consuming job.

The hospice industry continues to strive to bring dignity and personalization to end-of-life care. Some of the symptoms that can be managed by compounding include pain, nausea, vomiting, diarrhea, anxiety, and temperature.

The trained pharmacist can personalize the medicine for specific needs through dosage, strength, creams, suppositories, patches, and flavors. The hospice provider can work closely with the pharmacy to tailor a program to the patient's needs. Often, the unique medication that has been specially formulated for the patient will allow them to live a more comfortable life and minimize the sedation and other side effects from other routes.

Medication Packs

Hospice medications packs are provided for placement in the home to treat symptoms that may occur suddenly. This medication pack is usually placed in the refrigerator until needed. A call is usually placed by the caregiver to the hospice provider prior to opening and administering the pack. Instructions will always be given to the caregiver regarding the proper storage and administration of this bag/box. There are three types of adult comfort packs: comfort packs, cardiac comfort packs, and seizure comfort pack.

The comfort pack requires refrigeration and should include the following.

Medication	Form	Symptom
Acetaminophen	Suppositories	Pain, fever
Haloperidol	Oral	Agitation
Atropine	Under tongue	Terminal secretions
Lorazepam	Under tongue	Anxiety
Morphine	Under tongue, oral	Pain, Shortness of breath,
Prochlorperazine	Suppositories	Nausea, vomiting
Prochlorperazine	Tablets	Nausea, vomiting

The seizure comfort pack requires refrigeration and should include the following.

Medication	Form	Symptom
Acetaminophen	Suppositories	Pain, fever
Haloperidol	Oral	Agitation

Medication	Form	Symptom
Atropine	Under tongue	Secretions
Lorazepam	Under tongue	Anxiety, shortness of breath
Morphine	Under tongue, oral	Moderate to severe pain, SOB
Prochlorperazine	Suppositories	Nausea, vomiting
Prochlorperazine	Tablets	Nausea, vomiting
Lorazepam	Suppositories	Seizures

The cardiac comfort pack should not be refrigerated and should include the following.

Medication	Form	Symptom
Furosemide	Tablets	swelling, edema
Furosemide	Solution for injection	Swelling, edema
Nitroglycerin	Under tongue	Chest pain
Aspirin	Chewable	Chest pain
Morphine sulfate	Solution for injection	severe pain/SOB

Though I referenced some medications in the tables above, sometimes there are several medications available for each symptom.

Every hospice pharmacy across the United States should be able to fill the above appropriate comfort kits at the physician's order. This comfort kit should be in the home prior to the arrival of the patient and family. A person who is diagnosed with a terminal disease and given six months or less to live should never have to wait for a medication delivery. The family or caregiver needs to insist to the hospice that the medication arrive prior to the patient. You are the voice of your loved one. Sometimes you must use your voice to scream for what is needed. Scream all the way to the general manager of your hospice and then to JCAHO or CHAP—whoever regulates your hospice.

Scream

Agitation/Restlessness

Agitation is an uncomfortable state of extreme excitement. The person who is agitated may be experiencing pain, stress, or a fever. For a person with a terminal disease, the cause of agitation is often a symptom from the illness itself. Some of the health problems that can cause agitation are heart, lung, liver, and kidney disease. An older adult who has been in the hospital for delirium or an infection will experience agitation. Some medications such as amphetamines and steroids can cause someone to be agitated.

Any type of brain tumor can cause severe agitation. The important thing to remember is that your loved one is not him or herself. There are medications your hospice physician can prescribe to help ease this symptom, including the ones mentioned in the comfort packs. In addition to these, there are some I will list here, along with nonpharmaceutical ways to relieve agitation.

Chlorpromazine (Thorazine) is available by mouth. This medication also can be compounded into a cream or suppository.

Thorazine has sedative properties and contraindications for patients with Parkinson's disease.

Haloperidol is available in a concentrated form to be given sublingually. A patient who is agitated will sometimes spit it out. A pill form is also available, and the same result may occur. This medication may also be compounded into a cream to rub on the skin.

Risperidone is sometimes given for agitation and is available in pill form.

Lorazepam may also be given for agitation. Smaller dosages should be given to adults age sixty-five or older. Lorazepam is available in a cream.

There are also nonpharmacological therapies for agitation and restlessness. According to the National Institutes of Health, "the most important way to deal with agitation is to find and treat the cause." A person who is diagnosed with a terminal illness may often suffer from agitation due to a feeling that they have lost control over their life. Some anxiety is understandable, but agitation must be evaluated and treated properly. The above medications can help, but many times, agitation can be relieved by simply providing a calm environment with such calming features as a small, portable waterfall, soft music, a birdfeeder to watch the birds outside the window, or a light massage with their favorite lotion, day or night.

Anxiety

Anxiety is a feeling of being troubled or fearful. It also includes feeling tense or having nervousness. These feelings are common in people who are depressed or afraid. Many patients diagnosed with a terminal illness will have anxiety due to the unknown. The patient may be anxious about whether they are going to be in pain. It is the fear of the unknown that causes anxiety. I hope by the time you complete reading and working through the pages of this book your fears will be diminished.

There are many medications for anxiety your hospice provider has access to and your knowledge of them will help you understand.

There are several medications available for anxiety. Listed below are a few.

Medication	Form
Alprazolam	Pill
Clonazepam	Pill
Diazepam	Pill
Lorazepam	Pill, liquid, cream, capsule

The above medications will have a sedative effect. They are prescribed to calm the patient. Often, with patients over sixty-five, haloperidol will work when lorazepam does not.

Nonpharmacological Therapies for Anxiety

Remember that medical and nonmedical immediate relief may come from something as simple as breathing deep for a few seconds. You will hear news at this time that will cause you some anxiety. Take a deep breath first, find a good place in your mind, and relax. Light a candle, listen to some music and keep reading this informative book.

Please make sure the oxygen is turned off prior to lighting the candle.

Cachexia

Cachexia, or weight loss, is defined as a wasting away of both fat tissue and skeletal muscle. This occurs in many terminally ill patients. According to *The Merck Manual*, the primary cause of cachexia, (weight loss) is not decreased caloric intake. This loss of body mass occurs due to an increase in what is called tissue catabolism. Protein synthesis is decreased, and degradation is increased.

This means the body can no longer absorb the nutrients needed to sustain life as it did prior to illness, and weight loss is inevitable. The patient becomes weaker from lack of nutrition. The first response from the family is to insist their loved ones eat and drink something. The patient is unable for several reasons. One of the main reasons is nausea. There are some medications that may help and can be discussed with your hospice provider

Nonpharmacological Therapies for Weight Loss

Eliminate dietary restrictions and let the patient choose a favorite food and drink. Allow them to have what they want when they are craving it. Odor can increase nausea, so prepare odorless food and reduce the portion size.

Ask for assistance from the hospice provider regarding the emotional or spiritual topic of losing weight. One of the hardest struggles for families is watching their loved ones refusing or unable to eat. The social worker or chaplain can be a valuable resource during this time.

Medications for Constipation: Stool Softeners

Medication	Form
Docusate calcium	Pill
Docusate sodium	liquid, enema

Medications for Constipation: Stimulant Laxatives

Medication	Form
Bisacodyl	Tablet, suppository
Senna	Concentrate tablet, solution, syrup
Senna with docusate sodium	Tablet

Saline Laxatives

Medication	Form
Milk of magnesia	Liquid
Mineral oil	Liquid

Osmotic Laxatives

Medication	Form
Lactulose	Liquid
Magnesium citrate	Solution

Nonpharmacological Therapies for Constipation

Increase dietary fiber, if possible.
Increase fluid intake unless it would be detrimental to health due to kidney or heart disease.
Use natural laxatives such as smooth move tea, prune juice,
Ingest frozen Vaseline balls for high impaction. Roll a small amount of Vaseline into a pea-sized ball. Sugarcoat the balls and freeze. Administer them by mouth one to three times a day.

Cough

A cough is defined as a forceful expulsion of air through your throat with a short, loud noise. There are several medications available for a cough. The type of cough will determine what type of medication is appropriate to take. Your hospice provider will work with the hospice pharmacy to determine what is best based upon your symptoms. Listed below just for your knowledge are a few that are available.

Antihistamine-Antitussive Combinations

Medication	Form
Promethazine with codeine	Syrup
Promethazine with dextromethorphan	Syrup

Antihistamine-Antitussive-Decongestant Combinations

Medication	Form
Promethazine codeine phenylephrine	Syrup

Antitussives

Medication	Form
Benzonatate	Liquid-filled capsule
Dextromethorphan	Extended-release suspension
Homatrophine and hydrocodone	Syrup
Homatrophine and hydrocodone	Tablet

Antitussive-Expectorant Combinations

Medication	Form
Guaifenesin with codeine	Solution or syrup
Guaifenesin with dextromethorphan	Solution or syrup

Antitussive-Decongestant-Expectorant Combinations

Medication	Form
Guaifenesin with codeine and pseudoephedrine	Solution or syrup
Guaifenesin with dextromethorphan and phenylephrine	HCl solution

Expectorants

Medication	Form
Guaifenesin	Tablet
Guaifenesin	Solution or syrup
Sodium chloride	Nebulizer solution

Nonpharmacological Therapy for a Cough

> Encourage the patient to consume liquids.
> Reposition the patient to promote drainage.
> Provide cough drops for the patient.
> Use a humidifier in the room.

Delirium

Delirium is considered to be an acute confused state caused by rapid changes in brain function and is often related to some type of physical or mental illness. Usually, delirium persists for a short period of time and is reversible. Delirium is sometimes caused by conditions that do not allow the brain to get the required oxygen and substances it needs. Delirium involves a quick change from fatigue to alertness and can be confused with anxiety. The two symptoms require different medications, and the patient should be thoroughly assessed prior to the administration any medication so the right kind is given without over medicating. Some of the symptoms include

- changes in feelings and perception with a change in level of consciousness;
- changes in the type of movement, such as slowing down, with an increased need for sleep;
- confusion about time and place;
- disorganized thinking;
- nonsensical speech;
- inability to control bladder or bowel;
- personality changes, such as spontaneous anger, agitation, depression, irritability, or irrational happiness;
- difficulty concentrating; and
- uncontrollable movements triggered by the nervous system.

Medications Available for Delirium

Medication	Form
Chlorpromazine	Pill, intramuscular injection
Haloperidol	Pill, liquid, intramuscular injection, subcutaneous injection
Risperidone	Pill

Nonpharmacological Therapies for Delirium

Encourage drinking of fluids to replenish electrolytes.
Provide a quiet atmosphere at night with soft music.
Limit visitors during the evening hours.
Give baths during the morning hours.
Have enough lighting so the patient is familiar with his or her surroundings and does not panic. Family pictures and familiar paintings in the room can help.

Diarrhea

Diarrhea is described as abnormally frequent intestinal evacuations with loose stool. In a patient with a terminal illness, increases fatigue from the loss of electrolytes can occur.

Medications for Diarrhea: Absorbents

Medication	Form
Bismuth subsalicylate	Suspension

Medications for Diarrhea: Hypomotility Agents

Medication	Form
Diphenoxylate with atropine	Pill
Loperamide	Tablets, pill

Medications for Diarrhea: Antibiotics for Infectious Diarrhea

Medication	Form
Metronidazole	Liquid, tablet, capsule

Ellen J. Windham

Nonpharmacological Therapies for Diarrhea

Avoid stimulants such as coffee and nicotine.
Change the patient's diet temporarily to include clear liquids, bananas, rice, apples, and toast.

Dyspepsia

Dyspepsia is defined as indigestion—a pain in your stomach caused by difficulty digesting food.

Medications for Dyspepsia: Antacids

Medication	Form
Aluminum hydroxide/ magnesium hydroxide/ simethicone	Suspension
Simethicone	Liquid, pill
H2-receptor antagonists	
Ranitidine	Syrup, pill
Proton-pump inhibitors	
Omeprazole	Capsule

Nonpharmacological Therapy for Dyspepsia

Avoid being in a hurry when eating.
Avoid all spicy and greasy foods.
Exercise if you can.

Dyspnea is shortness of breath. This is the most uncomfortable and frightening symptom someone can have. The importance of effective medication and nonpharmacological treatment will be vital to the comfort of your loved one. The following is a list of the medications available to ease the discomfort.

Medications for Dyspnea: Anticholinergics

Medication	Form
Ipratropium bromide	Inhalation aerosol
Ipratropium bromide	Nebulizer solution

Medications for Dyspnea: Anticholinergic Bronchodilator

Medication	Form
Albuterol sulfate and ipratropium bromide	Nebulizer solution

Medications for Dyspnea: Sympathomimetic Bronchodilator

Medication	Form
Albuterol Sulfate	HFA inhalation aerosol, nebulizer solution, syrup, tablet
Opioids	Decrease the sensation of pain and shortness of breath
Morphine	Tablet, concentrated liquid

Nonpharmacological Therapies for Dyspnea

The patient should be allowed to position him- or herself in a manner that will make breathing easier. Sometimes that may be in a recliner.

Distractions can also help relieve shortness of breath, so get your loved one a television to watch or music to listen to.

A lightly blowing fan can assist with breathing.

Make sure the room is cool. If the patient is on oxygen, ask your hospice provider for longer tubing to move the concentrator into the hallway, as the concentrator puts out a lot of heat. Your equipment delivery person can help find a good spot.

Edema

Edema is a swelling of excess fluid that is confined inside the body's tissue. Edema can occur in almost any area of the body but the hands, arms, feet, ankles and legs are affected most of the time. Swelling arises when tiny blood vessels in the particular part of your body leaks fluid the result is fluid building in the surrounding tissue. The fluid buildup can be a result of several diseases, especially with terminally ill patients. Such as Congestive Heart Failure, Cirrhosis, Kidney Disease, Kidney damage and Weakness or damage to veins in your legs.

Medications for Edema: Loop Diuretics

Medication	Form
Bumetanide	Pill
Furosemide	Pill, IV

Medications for Edema: Potassium-Sparing Diuretics

Medication	Form
Spironolactone	Pill
Triamterene hydrochlorothiazide	Pill

Medications for Edema: Thiazide Diuretic

Medication	Form
Hydrochlorothiazide	Pill

Nonpharmacological Therapies for Edema

The patient's legs should be elevated above the heart when lying down. Exercising the legs helps the fluid to work back into the veins and the lymphatic path. Support stockings could provide a reduction in ankle swelling, as can elevating the legs when sitting in a chair for significant periods of time. The patient's diet should have significant reduction in salt.

Fever

Fever is a natural part of the body's own defense system. Although most information will tell you a body temperature above 98.6 degrees is not normal, there are discrepancies with this. The majority of people know what is normal for their own body temperatures. I have cared for patients whom I thought to have a slight fever at 99.1 degrees, only to have them tell me their normal temperature is 97.1. If you don't know the patient's normal temperature, a good rule most hospice providers use is 100.4 degrees. Everyone is different, so the best temperature guideline to use to determine whether intervention is needed is the patient's normal plus two degrees. Remember these interventions do not all have to be medication.

Medications for Fever: Antipyretics

Medication	Form
Acetaminophen	Pill, suppository
Aspirin	Pill, suppository
Ibuprofen	Pill
Ketoprofen	Capsule, gel

Nonpharmacological Therapies for Fever

The person may be cooled off with a cool cloth. The room should have all fans turned off when this is being done. Any extreme in the temperature should be avoided. Please never use ice to bring down temperature. It is uncomfortable to the patient.

I once worked for a great director of patient services who told all of her nurses that if she were on hospice and we put ice on her, she would come back and haunt us for the rest of our lives.

Peppermint oil or lemon essential oil can be useful in bringing down a fever. I have used them many times in hospice to bring down a high fever instead of giving medication rectally.

Hiccups

Hiccups are caused by a spasm that contracts the diaphragm and an intake of air that will suddenly close the vocal cords (glottis). Every person will experience hiccups at some time in life. A terminally ill person may experience them more often and for longer periods of time due to the disease itself. Hiccups at this stage can be very uncomfortable, and there are medications available through your hospice provider to treat them.

Medications for Hiccups: Anticonvulsants

Medication	Form
Valproic acid	Pill

Medications for Hiccups: Skeletal Muscle Relaxant

Medication	Form
Baclofen	Pill

Medications for Hiccups: Neuroleptics

Medication	Form
Chlorpromazine	Pill
Haloperidol	Pill, concentrated liquid

Medications for Hiccups: Compound Medication*

Medication	Form
Valproic acid	Suppository
Baclofen	Suspension, suppository
Chlorpromazine	Gel, concentrated liquid, suppository
Haloperidol	Gel, suppository

* Due to cost, you must request these medications from your hospice provider.

Nonpharmacological Therapies for Hiccups

Getting a light massage with lotion and relaxing music
Eating a teaspoon of sugar or honey
Sucking lemon wedges dipped in sugar, honey, or vinegar
Drinking a glass of water rapidly from the opposite side

Nausea

Nausea is a stomach distress with a distaste for food and an urge to vomit. Vomiting, or emesis, is defined as disgorging the stomach contents through the mouth. Nausea and vomiting are two of the symptoms of illness that can make an already ill person weaker. The timely manner in which this symptom can be stopped will have an impact on quality of life for your loved one. The following medications are available through your hospice provider.

Medications for Nausea: Anticholinergics

Medication	Form
Dicyclomine	Pill
Hyoscyamine regular release	Pill, sublingual
Hyoscyamine extended release	Pill
Scopolamine patch	Topical (behind ear)

Medications for Nausea: Antihistamine

Medication	Form
Hydroxine HCl	Pill
Hydroxine pamoate	Pill
Meclizine	Pill, chewable

Medications for Nausea: Benzodiazepines

Medication	Form
Lorazepam	Pill, sublingual, IV, intramuscular injection, subcutaneous injection

Medications for Nausea: Corticosteroids

Medication	Form
Dexamethasone	Pill, IV, intramuscular injection, subcutaneous injection

Medications for Nausea: Cannabinoids

Medication	Form
Dronabinol	Pill

Medications for Nausea: Dopamine Antagonists

Medication	Form
Perphenazine	Pill
Chlorpromazine	Pill, intramuscular injection, subcutaneous injection
Haloperidol	Pill, intramuscular injection, subcutaneous injection
Prochlorperazine	Pill, IV, intramuscular injection
Promethazine	Pill, rectal suppository, intramuscular injection

Medications for Nausea: Serotonin Receptor Antagonists

Medication	Form
Ondansetron	Pill, disintegrating tablet, oral solution, injection, suppository

Nonpharmacological Therapies for Nausea

Avoiding strong odors

Temporarily eliminating medications that make him or her nauseated

Relaxing by listening to music or watching television, for example

Keeping the room quiet and visitors to a minimum to avoid the patient needing to talk until the symptoms subside.

Ophthalmic Dryness

Ophthalmic dryness, or dry eyes, solution is available through your hospice provider, so I will list the kinds carried and covered by most hospice pharmacies.

Therapies for Ophthalmic Symptoms: Lubricants

Medication	Form
Artificial tears	Ophthalmic ointment, drops, solution

Therapies for Symptoms of Mouth and Throat Sores

Dental and Periodontal Agents

Medication	Form
Lidocaine	Oromucosal (viscous) solution
Nystatin Swish and Swallow	
Phenol	Oromucosal spray

Oromucosal Moisturizers

Medication	Form
Saliva Substitute (Biotene)	

The above saliva substitute is excellent at relieving dry mouth and throat.

Stomatitis

Stomatitis is an inflammatory disease of the mouth that causes irritation. Because the mouth is sore, try to eliminate or limit foods that require chewing or are acidic or dry. Salty foods can also hurt the patient's mouth.

All foods should be eaten at room temperature. Chilled and frozen yogurt in small portions is a high-protein snack and can be soothing to the inside of the mouth. Mouth care, including removal of dentures and a rinse with salt and baking soda in a weak solution, may help decrease soreness if done after each meal and prior to sleep.

Xerostomia

Xerostomia is defined as an abnormal dryness to the mouth. Treatments include ice chips, sugar-free gum, and pineapple chunks, as long as the patient is fully awake and sitting up. Providing good oral hygiene with a soft toothbrush and fluoride toothpaste can be valuable. If the patient is not awake, then Biotene Oral Balance placed on a damp toothette (which your hospice provider can provide) is the best at preventing mouth dryness.

Pain

Pain is defined as "a state of physical, emotional, or mental lack of well-being or physical, emotional, or mental uneasiness that ranges from mild discomfort to acute, often unbearable agony, may be generalized or localized, and is the consequence of being injured or hurt physically or mentally or of some derangement of or lack of equilibrium in the physical or mental functions (as through disease), and that usually produces a reaction of wanting to avoid, escape, or destroy the causative factor and its effects" (Pain, Merriam-Webster 2015).For a patient diagnosed with a terminal illness, we could not possibly describe the physical pain or the emotional pain this person has gone through in the years, months, or weeks leading up to this phase of life.

All I can do is make certain you are aware of the types of medications available to your loved one so you can make a knowledgeable request to your hospice provider. After medication is administered, pain management should not take more than twelve hours. If pain last more than twelve hours, then reevaluation should be done, and either the type or route of medication should be changed until relief occurs. The following medications are available through your hospice provider. Some are specific to the type of pain your loved one has. Some work well with other types of medications. Some of these medications will make your loved one sleepy at first until he or she becomes use to the medications. The dosages may have to be adjusted during the course of treatment.

Neuropathic Pain

Medication	Form
Carbamazepine	Tablets, suspension
Gabapentin	Tablets
Valproic acid	Tablets

Antidepressants

Medication	Form
Amitriptyline	Tablets
Despramine	Tablets
Nortriptyline	Tablets

Corticosteroids

Medication	Form
Dexamethasone	Tablets, IV, intramuscular injection, subcutaneous injection
Methylprednisolone	Tablets
Prednisolone	Tablets
Prednisone	Tablets

Local Anesthetics

Medication	Form
Dibucaine	Topical ointment
Lidocaine	Topical gel/jelly/ointment, transdermal patch

NMDA Receptor Antagonist

Medication | Form
Capsaicin | Topical gel

Miscellaneous

Medication | Form
Clonazepam | Pill
Clonidine | Pill
Mexiletine | Pill

Nociceptive Pain

Nociceptive pain includes somatic, visceral, and bone pain. Some of the medications available for this type pain through your hospice provider include the following.

Medications for Nociceptive Pain: Corticosteroids

Medication	Type
Dexamethasone	Pill, IV, intramuscular injection, subcutaneous injection
Methylprednisolone	Pill
Prednisolone	Pill
Prednisone	Pill

Medications for Nociceptive Pain: Nonopioid Analgesics

Medication	Form
Acetaminophen	Pill, liquid, suppository

Medications for Nociceptive Pain: Nonsteroidal Anti-inflammatory Drugs (NSAIDS)

Medication	Form
Diclofenac sodium	Pill
Ibuprofen	Pill
Naburnetone	Pill
Naproxen	Pill
Naproxen sodium	Pill

Medications for Nociceptive Pain: Long-Acting Opioids

Medication	Form
Fentanyl transdermal patch	Topical application
Methadone	Pill, liquid, concentrated
Morphine	Pill (cannot be crushed)

Medications for Nociceptive Pain: Short-Acting Opioids

Medication	Form
Codeine and acetaminophen	Pill
Hydrocodone & acetaminophen	Pill
Hydromorphone (Dilaudid)	Pill
Morphine instant release	Pill
Oxycodone instant release	Pill
Oxycodone & aspirin	Pill

Medications for Nociceptive Pain: Salicylates

Medication	Form
Aspirin	Pill, suppository

Medications for Nociceptive Pain: Compound Medications

Compound medication is a great alternative when the patient is unable to swallow any longer. The majority of hospice pharmacies all over the country have the capacity to compound any drug. The hospice provider you choose for your family member can verify this and fulfill your request to have certain medications given in a topical gel or cream, especially when there is nausea and vomiting with extreme pain. I will list a few you have access to with your hospice team.

Ativan/Benadryl/Haldol/Reglan can come in any combination the physician prescribes for your family member. It is a gel or a cream that is usually rubbed on the wrist, and it can manage the symptoms of nausea/vomiting, agitation, and anxiety.

Dexamethasone gel is considered a comfort medication in hospice. As stated previously, it is a corticosteroid that is very similar to the hormone produced in your adrenal gland that decreases swelling, heat, redness, and pain. Abruptly stopping this medication can cause some of the following symptoms: loss of appetite, nausea/vomiting, drowsiness, confusion, headache, fever, joint and muscle pain, peeling skin, and weight loss. If your loved one is unable to swallow the pill, ask for the gel.

Diazepam gel is used to stop seizures and calm agitation. The gel form of this drug works quickly and is easy to administer.

Diphenhydramine can be compounded into a cream to stop itching and help with sleep if needed.

Haloperidol gel works in the same manner as the liquid but can be administered by the family to stop nausea and agitation more quickly.

Ketoprofen gel is a NSAID. This gel works to stop pain, inflammation, and fever. It is a wonderful medication for a patient who is unable to swallow and cannot tolerate having a suppository.

Lorazepam gel works the same as the pill or liquid but is a less disturbing way to administer if the patient is sleeping.

Magic butt paste (hydrophilic ointment, lidocaine ointment, A&D ointment, and zinc oxide ointment) is used to relieve the pain of minor skin irritations, which occur often in patients confined to bed for extended periods of time.

Methadone suppositories can be administered if the patient is unable to swallow.

Metoclopramide gel/suppository can be administered if the patient is unable to swallow.

Morphine concentrated liquid is included in the comfort pack and is administered in small concentrated doses to relieve moderate to severe pain.

Morphine gel/suppository can be administered if the patient is unable to swallow or tolerate the concentrated form due to nausea and/or vomiting.

Naproxen suppository is an NSAID used to decrease pain and temperature.

Promethazine gel/suppository is an excellent medication to decrease nausea and vomiting.

Please make special note of this page of information on pain control. The majority of hospice pharmacies offer IV and continuous ambulatory delivery device (CADD) pumps for pain control. The CADD pump is a portable unit. The patient is administered a twenty-four-hour medication dosage, which is divided into an hourly rate, allowing the slow release of the medication at a controlled rate. A CADD pump could be appropriate for patients who

- are no longer able to tolerate oral medications,
- are unable to absorb gastrointestinal oral medications,

- experience severe nausea and/or vomiting, or
- have uncontrolled pain for which breakthrough medication is needed at a controlled rate at the patient's bedside.

The hospice physician can order an IV infusion and a CADD pump. You have to ask for this type of medication. As far as medications for the pumps, morphine and hydromorphone can be used at any dose the physician orders. In addition to the pain medication, lorazepam can be placed in the bag.

Please remember that you will often have to request these items.

Many families ask about hydration when their loved one can no longer swallow liquids. Unfortunately, this question has many answers, and all are complicated. This is the reason you must be informed about the options you and your loved one will have. There are many opinions on whether the patient is thirsty in the final stages of life. The best way for me to describe this is when it comes time when your loved one can no longer awaken or ask for water they will not require it. The use of the oral mouth swabs to gently moisten their lips and mouth will be the best way to avoid choking and aspiration.

Keep a chart much like the one below to remember what medications to give and how often.

Medications Taken Regularly	Amount	How Often	Last Taken
_____	_____	_____	_____
_____	_____	_____	_____
_____	_____	_____	_____
_____	_____	_____	_____

CHAPTER 12

MEDICAL EQUIPMENT AND USES COVERED BY MEDICARE

Durable medical equipment, also referred to as home medical equipment, may be needed to keep your loved one as comfortable as possible. The best time to discuss which equipment is necessary is during the admission to hospice, prior to signing consent forms. All of your medical equipment is provided by hospice, which owns or contracts with a company to supply what you need, and is ordered by the physician.

A person can develop a pressure ulcer, also called a decubitus or a bedsore that can occur for many reasons. Often it is because a person has been confined to a bed or chair for some time. A large number of people in the United States who are confined for extensive periods of time in the hospital and are transferred to rehabilitation centers and nursing homes are vulnerable. Many people who are admitted to either nursing homes or personal care homes, as much as 10 to 35 percent, have these sores. A bedsore is often caused from the weight of the body pressing the skin into a firm surface, causing blood supply to be cut off from the area of the body that is compromised. Bedsores can lead to many health complications and are very painful. Some infections that bedsores can lead to include bone and blood infections and infectious arthritis.

Some other problems that may create bedsores are shearing and friction, which cause the skin to stretch and the blood vessels to become obstructed. Moisture can also cause bedsores. Urine and stool that are allowed to sit very long on the person can cause the skin to break down faster than anything else. People who are paralyzed have an increased risk for bedsores because in addition to being unable to move themselves, they have decreased sensation in their skin. This is common with spinal cord injuries, dementia, and Alzheimer's. People with circulatory problems, diabetes, and some cancers are also at risk.

Sometimes, assisting your loved one to reposition in their bed is crucial. Bedsores are classified in stages. If you see a red area on a part of your loved one's body, that is stage one. From there, the wound progresses to a blister and is classified as stage two. The ulcer will then become a crater that will be beyond the skins surface and become a painful stage three. At this point, the ulcer will require intense treatment and turning of the person to heal. If not healed, the wound becomes stage four. At this stage, the muscle, bone, tendon, and joint are affected. The pain is severe because bacteria and infection set in.

Hospice companies have several mattresses at their disposal to order for your loved one. All the mattresses serve a great purpose, but I believe in being proactive. Why should a person, especially someone you love, not have the best to prevent bedsores, rather need to be treated after the damage has been done? They also have beds of all lengths and sizes available. Every person is different, but trust me—what you need is available. Please see the list below of the different types of mattresses available for hospice.

A gel overlay mattress will help provide minimal pressure reduction. This mattress is meant to fit over the existing mattress or the bed frame.

An alternating pressure pad is designed to be placed over the existing mattress and is a favorite of hospice companies. I have decided that the nurses in charge of ordering these for patients have never tried to sleep on one. They are cheap and uncomfortable.

A low air loss mattress is the mattress every patient on hospice deserves to have. This mattress will help prevent bedsores on someone in too much pain to be repositioned every two hours. It is comfortable, and the hospice companies will not order it for your loved one unless they already have a stage-three bedsore. If the hospice companies will order this mattress for a VIP patient, then everyone should have one.

Bariatric mattresses and beds are also an option. I bring up bariatric mattresses and beds because many patients I have cared for over the years could have benefitted from a larger bed. These beds also have low air loss mattresses. Cost is always going to be a factor with things of this world. My belief is that cost should never be a factor for a loved one who has gone through great suffering already.

Some people may experience anxiety regarding the use of oxygen. It is colorless, tasteless, and odorless gaseous element and is administered in various methods for therapy to manage and relieve symptoms of a host of illnesses.

The hospice physician will prescribe oxygen based on the diagnosis and current symptoms. It is a good idea for them to have the equipment company deliver the oxygen concentrator when the patient is admitted to hospice. The oxygen will be prescribed with portable, pressurized tanks and a machine called a concentrator, which runs on electricity. An oxygen concentrator has many advantages, including that that oxygen will never run out or have to be refilled. The only drawback is the concentrator requires electricity, so backup oxygen tanks are necessary. The backup tanks will be provided to you.

There are additional items you will need to operate the oxygen correctly. Among these is a nasal cannula, or plastic tubing that wraps over the patient's ears and two small prongs that fit into his or her nostrils. Sometimes the patient will need a face mask, which attaches to the oxygen tubing and fits over the nose and mouth. A mask is used if higher amounts of oxygen are needed or if the nose becomes irritated from the nasal cannula. There are precautions to take, and your hospice provider will help you understand.

Using oxygen may make the patient's lips, mouth, and nose become dry. It is all right to use products like aloe vera or Biotene Oral Balance for relief. Your hospice should have a supply of ear foams to prevent irritation. A piece of gauze under the earlobe will prevent irritation if the ear foams are not available.

Never use oil- or petroleum-based products like Vaseline, and never apply alcohol—it is combustible. Keep the oxygen away from heating sources and open flame, and make sure no one smokes in the room. Place signs on the door outside provided by your hospice or equipment company. Toys with electric motors, electric blankets, hairdryers, electric razors, and electric toothbrushes should not be near the oxygen.

Always tell your local fire department, electric company, and telephone company that someone in your home is using oxygen. Always post their numbers somewhere visible, like on the refrigerator. The electric company can restore power sooner to your home or neighborhood if the power goes out. Tell your neighbors, family, and friends, who can also help you if an emergency arises. They may possibly have a generator you can borrow. Always check the oxygen to make sure it is working. One way to do so is to briefly place the prongs of the cannula in a cup of water; air bubbles should be visible. Dry the cannula and then place it back into the nose.

Tubing for oxygen comes in many sizes with extensions. The oxygen concentrator puts out a great deal of heat when operating. Ask your hospice company for the equipment company to leave extra tubing with connectors to move the concentrator out in the hallway or away from the patient's room. If your loved one is already having difficulty breathing, the heat will make it worse. Try to keep the room cool or use a fan.

The nasal cannula is the adapter that fits into the nose to blow air from the oxygen concentrator or tank. The cannula is uncomfortable to many people. Try trimming the end with a pair of scissors so it does not go as far into the nose. Proper fit of oxygen is essential for someone having difficulty breathing. If the nasal cannula is too uncomfortable, or if the person is breathing through his or her mouth, you need to ask the hospice for an oxygen mask. The mask will fit around the nose and mouth with a strap for the back of the head to keep it on and in place.

A wheelchair is a chair that is mounted on wheels, especially for those who ill or are disabled. Wheelchairs come in all sizes.

Hospice

A shower chair allows a person to sit in the shower without the risk of falling.

A suction machine is a device for removing substances such as mucus when that interfere with breathing. It is portable and can be ordered among the medical equipment for hospice to be available in the home if needed. It is always best to have a sturdy table next to the bed with a bright light to ensure proper use. The suction machine will have what is called a yankauer. This piece fits just inside the mouth and does not cause discomfort or pain. It suctions all excess mucus from inside the mouth.

There may be times when the secretions are too deep in the lungs to suction. Some people refer to this as the death rattle. This sound can be very disturbing to the patient and the family. Studies show that death usually occurs twenty-four to forty-eight hours after this starts. The sound is more alarming than the actual event. Secretions build in the throat and lungs from the lack of strength to cough. There are ways for your hospice team to treat this symptom. Scopolamine patches behind the ear will help clear this in the beginning stages.

Because it takes several hours for the patches to begin working, make sure your hospice orders this medication before you need it. Atropine drops placed under the tongue will help also. Another solution to assist with breathing is to make sure the head is elevated and that the patient is in the most comfortable position for him or her.

CHAPTER 13

SIGNS AND SYMPTOMS OF THE JOURNEY HOME

Everyone is unique. Doctors and nurses can give you an educated guess about when the time of death on earth will occur, but it is just that—an educated guess. No one on earth knows the time for sure. I like to compare dying to birth. Both are actually births. It goes like this. When a baby is born, his or her heart beats fast, often 120 to 160 beats per minute. The baby has low blood pressure, sometimes as low as fifty over seventy. The baby has a breathing rate of thirty to fifty breaths per minute. The baby has what I call a small house to carry the spirit into this world. It is the only way here.

Hospice

When you die on this earth and are born in heaven, your heart rate can be 120 to 160 beats per minute, and your blood pressure is as low as fifty over seventy—or it may be so low it is unreadable. Your breathing rate is often thirty to fifty breaths per minute. The adult person dying has a large house, so it must stay here. The spirit makes the journey home. The house served its purpose on earth. I realize there are many books and opinions about what will begin to happen as far out as three months before death. My advice is not to focus on that. Live each day like it is your last. Be happy and have fun. Don't miss anything with your family and friends. God gives life, and only he can take it when it is time. People will tell you that your loved one will be waiting on someone or something. Here is my opinion on this topic.

I once cared for a young lady in her early forties. Her mom, husband, and grown children were present in the home. Prior to our arrival on crisis care, she had been in severe pain. We initiated a small portable Graseby pump because she could no longer swallow and the medications were not absorbing in her mouth. After a day on the pump, she was out of pain, but her husband felt her mother was keeping her alive. He forbade her mother to go into the bedroom for this reason.

Now, I didn't agree with this, so every time I needed help to turn her, I would ask Mom. Mom always gladly came to help so she could see her baby daughter. One night, after twenty-one straight nights of crisis care, I was so tired, and I said to God, "I am so tired, so please, please help her come home." As clear as day, I heard God say, "It's not about you."

Now, that being said, you have to understand that your loved one's death from this world is not necessarily about the nurses or you. It is about the loved one and God. As much as we think that it is all about us or that we have control, trust me—we don't. There is a time and purpose for everyone on this earth. No one comes here or leaves until God says it is time. Never stop a loved from talking to or seeing someone in their last days and hours. The only thing we take from this world is love and the good we have done. When we stand before God, we must be able to say that we did our best to serve mankind.

As discussed throughout this book, we are all different. God made us that way. So this is merely a guide. Your loved one may experience some of these symptoms, all of these symptoms, or only a few.

The symptoms can occur weeks before death, or they may occur sooner. Your hospice team will be able to guide you through these steps.

Confusion: Your loved one may seem confused at times, often about time and place. This is where the clock and calendar in the room are important. Confusion may be a due to changes in metabolism or to the effect of the medication keeping them comfortable. If your loved one is confused, explain again who you are and what you need for them to do in order to, for example, help keep his or her mouth moistened and lips from being dry. It is important for the body to be comfortable, especially the last weeks of life. Oxygen helps decrease confusion.

Restlessness: Your loved one may be awake day and night. He or she may walk and do repetitious things or be angry or tearful. Often, the patient will be angry with the person or people he or she loves the most. Many times, this is caused by the fear of not being able to awaken again if they go to sleep. Once your loved one has been awake for over twenty-four consecutive hours, it will be difficult to get him or her settled. Call your hospice provider immediately for help when this happens. Oxygen helps decrease restlessness. Assure your loved one everything is alright and attempt to distract them by discussing something they love. I once cared for an artist who was in this condition when I arrived to his home. I saw the beautiful paintings and began to ask about them. As he explain the meaning of each one, he calmed down.

Withdrawal from friends and family: Your loved one may only want to see a few people, perhaps due to a wish for others to remember him or her like that were before becoming ill. Your loved one is aware of the deterioration of his or her human body and only feel comfortable with immediate friends and family whose love is unconditional. It will be important for those who have the privilege of this enduring love to stay close, because that love is all we take with us when we leave this materialistic, earthly world.

Communicating with the spirit world: As mentioned in some of the final gift reflections, your loved one will often communicate with family members you cannot see, relatives who were very special and comforting to your loved one during childhood. He or she may also communicate with the angels who come to minister and prepare them for their journey home. I have been at bedsides where a patient spoke about a little child playing in the room. I don't know if it was a little boy or a little girl, but the child was always sweet and very quiet. My sister spoke to our mom and dad for two nights straight prior to leaving.

Food and fluids: This is probably the most difficult topic for families to understand and accept. I will explain to the best of my ability. As our human bodies prepare to leave this earthly world, we no longer require material things. This includes food and water to sustain life and energy to help our bodies work here. If your loved one is hungry or thirsty, he or she will let you know. If your loved one tells you he or she is hungry, then by all means, ask what he or she would like to eat. Sometimes there will be a burst of energy just prior to leaving this world where your loved one will eat and drink. If this happens, sit your loved one up in bed and allow him or her to eat slowly. If the patient asks for a favorite drink, even wine, please provide it, even if you dip a mouth swab into the liquid. The main thing to remember is not to force any food or water on you loved one. He or she could choke and die a horrible death. You love this person. Listen to what he or she wants. Remember—it's your loved one's journey. It's about him or her, not about you. Your time will come, and hopefully you will have passed these values to other members of your family, especially children.

Temperature changes: Your loved one may have increased temperature for many different reasons. As stated in a previous chapter, please don't use ice. An increase in temperature is a natural occurrence, and ice is very uncomfortable. I have seen so many nurses just insist on ice packs; evidently, they have never tried it on themselves. So if you are in doubt, try it before you place it on your loved one.

Use cool cloths, give a lukewarm bed bath with peppermint oil, turn on a fan, remove any heavy blankets, and ask your hospice provider for ketoprofen gel to place on your loved one's wrist. It is too difficult for some caregivers to administer suppositories.

Take your loved one's temperature twice a day, in the morning and in the evening, to make sure it doesn't get out of control. Most hospice providers have thermometers in stock at their offices.

Decrease in Urine: Sometimes, as the body systems begin to close down, the kidneys will stop producing urine as much. Even though the patient may no longer be drinking or eating, there will still be an output of fluid from the interstitial fluid of the body. A catheter may be needed if the bladder becomes enlarged and will not empty. Even as much as five hundred cubic centimeters of urine in the bladder can be uncomfortable and must come out. The urine will darken and have a foul odor due to the concentration of it. A special note here is that there should always be a bedside commode nearby. If your loved one wants to get up to urinate, then do whatever it takes to help him or her. Call family members or neighbors, and if no one is nearby, call the nonemergency number for the fire or police department. The first responders are always willing to help a hospice patient either to the bathroom or, sometimes, off the floor. I have called on them many times, and it has always been a quick response and free of charge. Our first responders are very compassionate.

Sleeping: There may be an increased need for sleep. It may seem as though it is difficult to wake your loved one. This is normal as the body prepares itself for the transition of the spirit home to God. Your loved one, though perhaps unable to open his or her eyes easily, is aware of your presence and can hear what you say. Hearing is the last of our senses to go, because it does not require energy. The others do: sight requires energy to open the eyelids, smell requires energy to sniff, taste requires energy to move the salivary glands on the tongue, and touch requires energy to move the extremity. Regarding touch, remember that touch is very important on your part. Sit with your loved one. Hold his or her hand and softly say how very much you love him or her and what a great job he or she did for God.

Breathing changes: Your loved one's breathing patterns may fluctuate differently each day. Normal breathing is sixteen to twenty breaths per minute. An irregular breathing pattern where the jaw actually moves up and down is known as Cheyne-Stokes. In the final weeks and days, your loved one may breathe ten breaths a minute or less with what is called apnea, or a ceasing of all breathing. This apnea can last from five seconds to sixty seconds. The person's mouth is usually open due to the relaxation of the jaw muscles. It is all right to leave the oxygen on, because the patient continues to get some air from it. Often, the breathing may be just the opposite, and breathing rates may climb to forty to sixty breaths per minute. This is where your hospice provider can advise the best solution to help with the symptoms.

Congestion and secretions: When you hear the term "death rattle," this is the sound that refers to. First and foremost, please remember that the majority of the time, this may never happen. If it does, it is usually twenty-four to forty-eight hours prior to death of the body. You loved one is not suffering. The sound may cause you to distress, so your hospice provider will help you through this. Suction machines should already be in the home. Now, I have worked for large national hospice companies with certain physicians who will not order the medication for congestion. Some believe the medication will not work and often times it will not. There are patients the medication will work. This is where you scream as loud as you can if you want your hospice provider to do something more to help.

You are the only voice for your loved one. You have to take charge and make the hospice do what it promised. Do not be intimidated by anyone. Do request everything you need and ask that it be delivered to your home or wherever home for your loved one is.

Mottling: This term is used to describe a discoloration in of the skin. It is caused from a lack of oxygen to that area. Usually, mottling will occur on the extremities farthest from the heart. The feet will turn a slight purple color and feel cold. The knees and hands may also be affected. This is not painful to your loved one. If your loved one doesn't have a fever, applying an additional blanket will be comforting. Remember this when you are so tired emotionally and physically that you feel you cannot go on.

I know God will not put any extra on me than I can bear.

I only wish he did not trust me so much.

We Never Know

We never know what life has in store for us, what's around the next bend, or what will go well or go through. Time ticks away, and we all have a choice: to wring our hands or to pick ourselves up and say, "Next!" We can look from the bottom side up or the top side down. We can grow in despair or we can grow in spite of fear. We can close life down, or we can open life up. We can angrily curse life for treating us poorly, or we can be grateful for what we do have and whose we are. We can begin loving those around us, regardless of timing or any transgressions. We can say thank you to life, for it means we have another day. We can reach out for our Savior, who is always there and never stumbles. We can speak God's promises until they become reality. We can learn how to praise and walk in His light. We can enjoy those around us and let God be our giver of joy. For this we do know. What the enemy meant for evil, God transforms for good. For we are his, and we are dearly loved.

CHAPTER 14

MY JOURNEY TO HOSPICE

My journey began several years ago at a time when I was unemployed. I became depressed and could not understand how the job I had held could be gone. I had worked in sales and public relations in Houston, Texas. Although I enjoyed sales, I loved the creation and implementation of programs for the children's hospitals in the Texas Medical Center Houston/Galveston. I also worked on some children's programs across the United States. I lost that job one day just out of the blue. I felt like I had lost my calling in life when this happened. The thousands of children I had helped would no longer benefit from the wonderful, positive programs. I was devastated and could not understand why this had happened. I found myself praying, "If there is nothing left for me to do, then let me come home."

I was lying on my bed and crying out to Jesus. For a moment of time, my spirit was in his presence. I did not visually see him, but I knew it was the living God. I knew because the peace and love was overwhelming. There is no feeling like it on earth. As much as you love someone, if you multiplied it by infinity, there would be no comparison to how much God loves us. There were words spoken but not by mouth. Everything was mental, and it was like I knew why I had been sent to earth and what I was supposed to do.

The Lord revealed to me a line of spirits. Now, this line went on for what seemed like forever. There were so many spirits standing there that it was impossible to see the end of the line. The spirits looked like they had been waiting there a long time, but I did not know why.

I could not see the end of the line. I could see the beginning and the first few spirits. The first few were extremely happy and excited. I did notice one thing about the spirits. They were all the same size and shape, and they had no age, color, or sex. Then, I heard God ask me, "You want to come back here? Look how long this line is." I kept looking at the line—some of these spirits looked like they had been standing a long time. I said, "No, I don't want to stand in that line. It's too long."

God revealed to me that the spirits were coming to earth. I could actually see them. Although the line was long, the spirits were moving quickly. There were occasions when a spirit did not get to go. I could sense disappointment in them but only briefly. They would get to come to earth the next second. So all the spirits in line were coming to earth, but only when God said they could. No one left without him saying so.

God said to me, "My work is on earth, and I want you to do these three things: be patient, don't get angry, and have fun."

"No problem," I said. "That will be a piece of cake. I can do that."

In an instant, I was back. There was no tunnel or bright light. My journey with God was in the blink of an eye. There are many disbelievers of God and of our purpose on this earth. There will be many people who will doubt what happened to me. For that reason, I am going to give you some background on my childhood.

My mom and stepdad married when I was two years old. My siblings and I grew up in the 1950s and 1960s, in Houston, near what is called the third ward. This was a time when the country suffered from racial prejudice unlike anything people see today. We were taught as children to be prejudiced against people who were different, so as we grew older, we held the same values. I held these prejudices until the Lord revealed to me the line of spirits. As I said, all the spirits in this place were the same size and shape with no age, color, or sex. When I returned to my earthly body, every bit of prejudice was gone. There is not anything or anyone who can take hate and prejudice away that quickly and entirely but the almighty God through Jesus Christ.

I don't know why he decided to reveal this to me. I don't think I am any more special than anyone else. I have made mistakes in my life before my journey to heaven and have made some since. All I try to remember is that we are here for a reason and for a very short time. We have good days and bad days. We are here to help each other and do the best we can without causing anyone intentional pain. Soon after this experience, I was sitting with my sister, Cathy, in church. Our pastor's sermon was about the inconceivable need in the world for help. He asked if anyone would be willing to take up his or her cross and go fish.

I heard a quiet voice in my heart that said yes. I was a salesperson with public relations skills. I could not figure out how I could help anyone. My education consisted of GED, what my sister called a "good enough degree." I was in the US Air Force, and since my tour of duty was in peacetime, I did not leave America. Soon after the sermon, my oldest daughter, Tina, suggested I try medical assisting school. I had quit school at an early age and could not consider myself smart enough to attend any type of college. Tina insisted and actually drove me to the school. I continued to be skeptical about actually attending a business school to learn anything about medicine. Once there, the school counselor informed me of the available courses and the required entrance exam.

Hospice

I went back to the school the following week and took their entrance exam, and to my surprise, I passed. The program was a year long, and I went through each course of study with highest marks. I studied hard and passed the program with a 4.0 GPA. I could not believe how wonderful I felt. It seemed as if everything was coming together in my life and God was finally showing me which direction to take.

I began to research and found a seminar explaining the work of medical missionaries in Tyler, Texas. When I returned home, my friend at the Department of Veterans Affairs ask me to help care for a dignitary who was ill and far from home of Guatemala. The man was a veteran of the US Army Intelligence and Security Command with service in the Korean War. He was very weak and needed someone to help him to his appointments at the hospital. It was this man who put me in contact with an organization to serve.

My two children were grown. I answered my calling, sold my home for cash in thirty days, made certain my children were stable and secure, gave everything away, picked up my cross, and was ready to go. My mission was to Swaziland, Africa. The week prior to my departure, I received a phone call that my voyage was cancelled due to complications and that the mission board would get back to me.

I began to wonder if I had been abandoned, because now I was without a place to go and without a home. Just before I moved out of the house, the board called and asked if I would consider going to Israel. I said yes excitedly and prepared for my new journey to serve God in the Holy Land.

My mission was in Bethany, Israel, a city on the West Bank. Upon my arrival to Ben Gurion Airport, I took a cab from Tel Aviv to Jerusalem. I was traveling on a tourist visa, the only way to gain access to my destination due to restrictions imposed on missionaries. My assignment was in the children's section of a hospital in Bethany.

This trip would change my life over and over again. I was a medical assistant, led by God, traveling across the world without knowledge of the area I was about to enter. I did not miss the luxuries of home as I knew it, but I had a hard time adjusting to the lack of basic needs. I did not have the same access to food and water as we have in America. I traveled into the Old City of Jerusalem on the weekends.

Nearby, at Jaffa Gate, there was an Internet café where I could get a cold Coke to drink and e-mail home. I did have a big advantage over tourists visiting the Holy Land. I was traveling alone and entered places the tourists couldn't for security and safety reasons. It wasn't that I was brave; I simply did not realize my life could be in danger. I can tell you that I was never afraid the entire time I traveled and worked in the Middle East. The phrase "God takes care of drunks and fools" crossed my mind many times upon my return, and I can tell you I don't drink.

My work in Bethany was rewarding and, at times, difficult. The children had been abandoned by their families and suffered from multiple handicaps. They had caregivers at the hospital who did the best they could. The children were starved for attention, most unable to sit up or walk. Some have wheelchairs, but most do not. Medical volunteers from nations around the world go help as much as possible, but travel to the region has become increasingly difficult.

The adults and children were in such need of food, clothing, bedding, medical care, and medicine. One day, I went into New Jerusalem and purchased the largest portable swimming pool I could find. I thought being in the water would help the children's muscles and that they could have fun. The nurses and I set it up on the covered day porch. The children were so excited and did have hours of fun.

I spent a few weeks trying to figure out what on earth God wanted me to do so badly that he wanted me to give up everything and travel halfway around the world. I became angry—one of the stages of grief, as Elizabeth Kubler-Ross explained. "Why me?" I asked God. "Why did you pick me to come here?" I began looking for him. I went everywhere in the Old City of Jerusalem—the Church of the Holy Sepulchre, the garden of Gethsemane, the Mount of Olives, and the area of King David's castle. He was nowhere to be felt or found. Remember—I was traveling by myself without an American connection in the country. The only instruction I had was from the matron at the hospital, who had told me to never be out after dark, as it was too dangerous.

As I walked, I could see people in the distance having the most incredible experience of worship and song and praise. I thought, *Wow, that is really amazing.* I had nothing and did not understand why. Just as I was about to give up, it happened.

I was in the day room one morning waiting for a little girl I had met and played catch with. The person bathing her brought her into the room and dropped her onto the thin mat in front of me, and I picked her up and held her. As I did, I looked into her eyes and saw tears falling from them. I remember staring into her eyes without a blink from her or myself, and as I did, I saw the spirit of the living God. I took a deep breath, and my spirit said to him, *Oh, there you are. I have been looking everywhere for you!* The funny thing is that since the experience of seeing Jesus Christ in the eyes of this child, I see him in every patient I now have the privilege of caring for.

It wasn't long after this event when God opened every door for me to come home. I had no idea what was waiting for me. I arrived at Ben Gurion Airport in Tel Aviv by taxi. The driver and I were stopped prior to entering the airport. The Israelis wanted my passport. The taxi allowed them to see it, and we proceeded to the terminal. I was early to my flight, so I decided to have something to eat. Of course, I had five suitcases to keep up with as well. After eating and gathering all of my worldly belongings, I proceeded to the British Airways ticket counter.

I was a few hours early checking in, so I was first in line and patiently waited for the ticket counter agents to arrive. All of a sudden, I looked up and saw two men in suits, each accompanied by a soldier carrying a submachine gun. The men then walked up to me of all people. To my surprise, they introduced themselves as Israeli intelligence and demanded that I hand over my passport and airline ticket and that I come with them. I said, "No, thank you, I am waiting for my flight home to the United States." They escorted me to a little room, took my luggage, and searched me. I thought, *Well, this is just great. Why me, Lord? I came over here just as you led me to.*

For the next four hours, I answered questions the best I could. A social worker I met in Bethany had given me a Scripture. It was written on a small piece of paper and was the only thing I had in the pocket of my scrubs. The scripture was not written in its entirety, but only a portion. It was taken in part from the Amplified Bible, Hebrew 13:5.

For he has said, "I will never desert you nor give you up nor leave you without support, nor will I in any degree leave you helpless, nor will I forsake or let you down or relax My hold on you assuredly not!"

As the questions continued, all I could do was pull this Scripture out of my pocket. They took everything I owned into another room and then took everything apart, including my clothes. I underwent three body searches. Each time they found something in my luggage that they found suspicious, they would ask me to explain.

I felt like a criminal but could not understand why. I began apologizing to God for complaining so much about the lack of food and ice water. When I asked them to call the American Consulate, they laughed and said no, and I began to feel like I might be in trouble for something.

I started to think, *I might be in jail soon with the rats—and no one knows where I am right now.* I began bargaining with God: *I get it, and when I get home, I will go back to school and promise to work for you for the rest of my life. Right this minute, my path and ability is unclear to me, but I know you will reveal it when the time is right. I will take one day at a time and live that day to the fullest with faith and not fear.* After four hours of interrogation, as quickly as I was detained, I was released and escorted to my plane.

I knew in my mind and heart I was released because of God. I also knew I had to fulfill the promise I had made. When my plane landed, I was home in Houston, Texas. My family was there to greet me even though my plane was fifteen hours late. My sister was standing there holding a sign they had made. It read Welcome Home to America, Land of the Free and Home of the Brave—Home of Air Conditioning, a Soft Bed, Ice Water, and Cold Vitamin D Milk.

After many hours of rest, I made a visit to the Israeli Consulate with my mom to inquire as to why I had been detained and why the officers had been so rude. The answer from the Consulate General helped me realize that things are not always as they seem. He stated, "In the first place, you were in the country illegally on a tourist visa. You were not supposed to be working on the West Bank. Bethany is across the checkpoint and in Palestinian territory. You are a female traveling alone. Our guards have been watching you since you landed in Israel." He told me that a week before I returned to Ben Gurion Airport to depart for America, a leader of Hamas had been killed by Israeli forces, and they were expecting retaliation in the form of a bomb. They thought *I* had that bomb. I apologized for any inconvenience I had caused in my ignorance of my surroundings and promised to never leave the United States of America again.

I started my life over and began the path to the work I had promised to do. I lived with my sister for a while and studied every day. I knew that in order to fulfill my mission, I would need an education. I enrolled in nursing school, was admitted, and graduated on the dean's honor list. I loved nursing—especially at the Department of Veterans Affairs. I am a veteran of the US Air Force myself, so it was an honor to care for my fellow veterans. I would soon learn that this was not the plan God had for my life.

I was led to go back to school and further my education. In the meantime, a dear friend of mine called me and told me his brother was sick and had been sent home to die. When he had retired and moved to Galveston, he had suffered renal failure and was undergoing dialysis.

I dropped everything and went to Galveston. At this time, I did not have any experience with hospice. Hospice is a field completely opposite of everything we are taught in medicine. We are taught to save life at all costs. Hospice is about creating a symptom-free and pain-free environment. I sat up with him all night. I said the rosary for him over and over again and just knew he could hear me. My friend left this world and went home the next morning.

It was at that moment I knew what I was called to do. What an awesome privilege to care for people as they take their last breaths on this earth. I began working for an agency in 2002 as a crisis care nurse at patients' bedsides. A few years later, I went to work directly for a hospice in Houston, Texas. I worked twelve-hour

Hospice

shifts and was the only night nurse working crisis care for the company. I learned so much from some very special people. The compassion and knowledge of hospice that many of the nurses exhibited to patients and families far surpassed the requirements of their job description.

I was able to care for many patients and families. I was taught that if you have one patient to care for on hospice service and twenty family members in the home, please always remember you have twenty-one patients. The loss of a loved one is the most stressful time of their lives. There is no room for any type of mistake. If a patient has a symptom that is not controlled within six to eight hours, then the type of medication and possibly the route must be changed. My years with this hospice made up some of the most rewarding times of my life.

It came to pass that I would be called toward a new direction in life. My daughter lived in a city just north of Dallas, Texas. She had two daughters and needed help. I left Houston to help her for a short time—and ended up staying for six years. While I was there, I became employed with a different hospice organization in Dallas. I also went back to school. I graduated cum laude with a degree in psychology and began planning to write this book.

I decided to enroll in a bachelor's program at the University of North Texas. I loved school and graduated in the top 5 percent of the school, which had an enrollment of thirty-six thousand students. My graduating GPA was 3.9.

It was time to move back to Houston, so I took a transfer with my company. My granddaughter had received her bachelor's in kinesiology when I received mine in gerontology. Courtney also received a scholarship to a University of Houston graduate program. We rented an apartment in the Texas Medical Center and lived together for a year. My sister was diagnosed with cancer for the second time.

Families do not know and cannot be expected to know all about hospice. It is my prayer the information in this book will help you and your loved one understand. These are the rules as mandated by government, for-profit, and nonprofit organizations that hold the hospice industry accountable. You have the right to know what is available for you or your loved one. Knowledge is power. We never stop learning until the day we die in this world and are born in the next.

I want you to use the information in this book as a guide to learning everything you can about your family member's or friend's diagnosis. Fight for your loved one to have everything he or she needs to be comfortable. Fight so that every minute your loved one spends on this earth counts, and don't let anyone take that away from you or your loved one. When the time comes to say good-bye, you can do it knowing you have done everything in your power to help, so have fun and be as happy as possible.

CHAPTER 15

FINAL GIFTS FROM PATIENTS AND FAMILIES

A final word from a loved one is the most precious gift anyone can receive. I have been at the bedside and heard patients' words just before taking their last breaths. They opened their eyes to whisper to their loved ones and said, "I love you." I tell you this so that you will focus on today, on this minute you have together. Do not focus on the disease or what the doctor tells you regarding the amount of time your loved one may have left before death.

A sponge bath with a light massage can be as effective as medication. I once cared for a patient in an assisted living facility. When I arrived, I noticed she was scratching her head. I asked her when the last time she had a hair shampoo was. She said, "Oh, I just cant remember." I gave her a spa bath (a bath with each extremity wrapped in a towel), shampooed her hair, and gave her a very gentle massage with lotion. When finished, I asked her how she felt. My patient, at eighty-nine years old, replied, "I feel like I have already died and gone to heaven."

Your loved one may experience things that you may have a difficult time understanding if you have never experienced someone dying. For instance, as I stated earlier in the book, someone who has passed before is always waiting for the dying loved one. He or she may see and talk to a loved one who has been gone for a long time.

I once cared for a lady in McKinney, Texas. She was lying in her own bed. Her daughter and I were standing at the end of the bed talking. The mom opened her eyes and said, "Would the two of you please move? I cannot see those three pretty precious ladies at the end of my bed." We immediately moved for her.

One of my favorite patients to care for was a lady who lived at an assisted living facility. She had come home from the hospital around three in the afternoon. At three in the morning, she was still sleeping, so I began to sing a song to her. Now, I don't sing well. The song was "Rudolph the Red-Nosed Reindeer." On the third verse, she opened her eyes, looked at me, and said, "Do you have a job, or is your only job to entertain me?" My response to her was that was my only job. She laughed out loud and then took a bath.

Some of the most important and enlightening things I have learned over the years are the following. If it is our time to go home, that's great—if not, then faith in God, a positive attitude, family, friends, and good doctors are essential. We must live each day like it is our last.

Have fun, be patient, and don't get angry—it is an excellent way for all of us to live.

My sister, Cathy, and the love of her life, Kirk, moved to Austin, Texas, and commute to MD Anderson Cancer Center every three months now.

Cathy met a new friend by the name of Eileen. They walk, talk, and have fun every day that ends in *y*. I met Eileen on a visit I took to Austin. She had walking poles to help her stay balanced. I said, "What a great concept." She wrote the story below and gave me this picture to share with all of you.

"I had an amazing experience with the kind and gentle hospice workers here in Austin when my stepfather passed away several years ago. Their approach to the dying process was very comforting, as we will all die one day. One of the workers told my mother and me that we should all look at his death as a celebration. We all await the arrival of a newborn baby with great excitement and hope for the new life that is about to be born. When someone is dying, she told us, we should view it as a gift that we get to share in this experience with our loved one. The workers' kind and loving words and excellent care of my stepfather offered us great comfort."

REFERENCES

"About CHAP." *Community Health Accreditation Partner.* Accessed 2015. http://www.chapinc.org/why-chap003f/about-chap.aspx

Amplified Bible, Hebrew 13: 5-6 by The Lockman Foundation www.Lockman.org

"Durable Medical Equipment." *Medicare.gov.* Accessed October 14, 2014. http://medicare.gov/coverage/durable-medical-equipment.html.

"Funeral Rule." United States Federal Trade Commission, www.ftc.gov/

Gilley, Judy. "Intimacy and Terminal Care." March 1, 1988. http://bjgp.org/content/38/308/121

"How Hospice Works." *Medicare.gov.* Accessed September 22, 2014. http://www.medicare.gov/whatmedicare-covers/part-a/how-hospice

Lasagna, Louis. "Hippocratic Oath." Home. Accessed October 10, 2015. http://guides.library.jhu.edu/bioethics.

Lamers, W. M. "Hippocratic Oath." *Macmillan Encyclopedia of Death and Dying.* Accessed July 9, 2015. http://www.encyclopedia.com

"Med Terms." *MedicineNet.com.* Accessed October 22, 2014. http://www.medicinenet.com

MedlinePlus Medical Encyclopedia. Accessed October 22, 2014. http://www.nlm.nih.gov.

Medical Dictionary. *Merriam-Webster.* Accessed October 11, 2014. http://www.nlm.nih.gov

"Moments of Life." *National Hospice and Palliative Care Organization.* Accessed October 27, 2014. http://www.nhpco.org/press-releases

Name A Star Live. Accessed October 27, 2014. http://www.nameastarlive.com/faq.asp

"Oxygen Therapy Supplies." Venture Respiratory Inc. Accessed October 27, 2014. http://www.ventureresp.com

"Pain." Merriam-Webster.com. Accessed October 10, 2015. http://www.merriam-webster.com/dictionary/pain.

Rhymes, Jill A. "Barriers to palliative care." *Cancer Control* 3, no. 3 (1996) 230-6.

Riely, Gregory J. "Cancer Care during the Last Phase of Life." ASCO.org. 1998. Accessed October 10, 2015. http://www.asco.org/

Ross, Elisabeth Kubler. "The Grief Cycle." http://www.recover-from-grief.com/kubler-ross-stages-of-grief.html

Taylor, Phyllis B. "Understanding Sexuality in the Dying Patient." *Nursing* 13, no. 4 (1983): 54–55.

"The Gerontologist." Referral and Timing of Referral to Hospice Care in Nursing Homes: The Significant Role of Staff Members. 2008. Accessed October 10, 2015. http://gerontologist.oxfordjournals.org/content/48/4/477.short

"The Joint Commission." Accreditation, Health Care, Certification. 2008. Accessed October 10, 2015. http://www.jointcommission.org/

"Understanding Hospice - An Underutilized Option for Life's Final Chapter — NEJM." New England Journal of Medicine. July. Accessed October 10, 2015. http://www.nejm.org/doi/ref/10.1056/NEJMp078067#t=references.

"United States Federal Trade Commission, www.ftc.gov " Funeral Rule.

"What Is Compounding?" Professional Compounding Centers of America. Accessed October 2014. http://www.pccarx.com

ABOUT THE AUTHOR

Ellen Jane Windham is a nurse with an associate of science degree in psychology and a bachelor of applied arts and science with certification in applied gerontology. She has more than fifteen years of experience at bedsides and has worked with more than ten thousand patients on service with hospice who have completed their missions and made it home peacefully, surrounded by family and friends.

It is my hope and prayer that this book will encourage and empower patients and families as they take one minute at a time, one hour at a time, one day at a time.

CPSIA information can be obtained
at www.ICGtesting.com
Printed in the USA
FSOW01n1642061215
14044FS